After the Good News

After the Good News

Progressive Faith Beyond Optimism

Nancy McDonald Ladd

Skinner House Books
Boston

www.skinnerhouse.org

Printed in the United States

Cover design by Kathryn Sky-Peck
Text design by Suzanne Morgan

print ISBN: 978-1-55896-828-8
eBook ISBN: 978-1-55896-829-5

6 5 4 3 2
23 22 21 20 19

Library of Congress Cataloging-in-Publication Data

Names: Ladd, Nancy McDonald, 1978- author.
Title: After the good news : progressive faith beyond optimism / Nancy McDonald Ladd.
Description: first [edition]. | Boston : Skinner House Books, 2019. |
    Includes bibliographical references.
Identifiers: LCCN 2018046721 | ISBN 9781558968288 (pbk.)
Subjects: LCSH: Public worship. | Liturgical reform.
Classification: LCC BV15 .L33 2019 | DDC 230/.91—dc23 LC record available at https://lccn.loc.gov/2018046721

We gratefully acknowledge permission to reprint the following: lines from "Lift Every Voice and Sing," written by James Weldon Johnson and J. Rosamond Johnson, published by Edward B. Marks Music Company, all rights administered by Round Hill Carlin, LLC; "The Gates of Hope" by Victoria Safford, reprinted by permission of author.

To the Ladds—Jon, Ruth, and Josiah.
I love you past the edges of everything.

To the Bull Run Unitarian Universalists and River Road
Unitarian Universalist Congregation, for putting up with me
until I figured out how to work the copy machine.

And to the McDonalds—Mark, Ann, and Karra—
for being beloved thorns in the side of the sanctimonious and the
self-righteous—in the shadow of the dead utopias and beyond.

The Gates of Hope

Our mission is to plant ourselves at the gates of Hope—
Not the prudent gates of Optimism,
Which are somewhat narrower.
Not the stalwart, boring gates of Common Sense;
Nor the strident gates of Self-Righteousness,
Which creak on shrill and angry hinges
(People cannot hear us there; they cannot pass through)
Nor the cheerful, flimsy garden gate of
"Everything is gonna be all right."
But a different, sometimes lonely place,
The place of truth-telling,
About your own soul first of all and its condition.
The place of resistance and defiance,
The piece of ground from which you see the world
Both as it is and as it could be
As it will be;
The place from which you glimpse not only struggle,
But the joy of the struggle.
And we stand there, beckoning and calling,
Telling people what we are seeing
Asking people what they see.

—Victoria Safford

Contents

Introduction

A Realist Spy among the Optimists

> I want to suggest a strong note of reserve, of pessimism, of the ambiguous which it seems to me are of the very nature of life today. . . . And then to ask: In spite of it all, what are we to do with our lives? A question which seems to me a peerless source of freedom to the one who dares pose it with seriousness. It seems clear by now; anything short of confronting this question ends up sooner or later in a suffocating dead end.
>
> —Daniel Berrigan[1]

As a child in a rural Midwestern town, I grew up in the shadow of two dead utopias.

As a preacher in a progressive American Protestant tradition trying to speak an honest word among the raging storms, bullet-trails, and supremacy systems of this nation, I work in the ever-reaching shadow of another.

This experience of living and working amid these dead utopias has shaped me as a religious leader since before I entered seminary at the beginning of a new century—part of a wave of young Generation X pastors striving to reinterpret and to pass on the received traditions of our respective faiths.

Though not even twenty years have passed since the beginning of this century, in many ways the early 2000s felt like an entirely different era for progressive religion in America. Perhaps more accurately, it felt like the end of one—the waning days of a time when religion itself wasn't such an antiquated and questionably relevant force in American culture. It was the end of a time when seminary education still assumed continued growth and vitality in the mainline and left-of-center churches, when Nazis still wore white hoods instead of white polo shirts, and "onward and upward forever" was the liberal preacher's mantra of historical progress that many of us still at least sort of believed in.

Even just two short decades ago, the utopian dream of late-twentieth-century American liberal religion centered around the greatness of human capacity, the vastness of God's unending love, and the ultimate triumph of scientific advancement and moral progress. The immediate predecessors and role models who gave rise to the preachers and pastors of my generation quoted Amos to remind us that one day justice would indeed roll down like waters and righteousness like a mighty stream. They helped us to believe that great people with a great call, anointed by a loving but distant God, could create something akin to heaven on earth.

Sometimes, the path to that utopian dream seemed to be paved by nothing more than the exertions of our own energy and a smattering of grace to fill in the cracks where our efforts fell short.

The late-twentieth-century liberal religion I encountered in seminary was a faith that believed in people. Our churches believed in us. Our faith taught us that true moral advancement for the culture as a whole was possible. Some among us said it was inevitable. And yet, something about the prospect of preaching a fundamentally optimistic gospel of expansive human capacity and liberal progress left an empty, aching place inside my gut. Something was missing in the good news I was learning to preach.

When I entered seminary, I was fresh off a short period of vocational discernment in a Dominican convent and just on the other side of a degree in theology at a progressive Jesuit university. As a lifelong liberal Catholic, I was steeped clear through with liberation theology. I had even bent my knees at the very altar once presided over by Archbishop Oscar Romero.

I knew, however, that my professional religious calling did not lie within progressive Catholicism. The reasons are not too mysterious—it turns out I wasn't supposed to be a nun.

Armed with this difficult and liberating truth, yet still informed by the poetry and pain of the Catholic liturgy, I went looking for a way to be faithful to my calling. I sought a religious context that would make room for the liberationist theologies that formed me but that would also push me out on some new path.

So, I packed up my spiritual treatises by Thomas Merton, my undergraduate thesis on sixteenth-century female mystics, and my poster of Dorothy Day and made my way gratefully into the wide-open arms of Unitarian Universalism—which has been my religious home ever since.

A few short years later, I enrolled in seminary. I walked the halls of the liberal Protestant academy with gratitude and even abundant relief. I spent my days absorbing the unique history and theology of twentieth-century religious progressivism, while working to integrate myself into this family of faith that had been gracious enough to make a place for me.

In many ways, the transition from progressive Catholicism to liberal Unitarian Universalism was not difficult at all. The theologically diverse, justice-minded Catholicism of my upbringing and the progressive Protestant reform tradition of my chosen path didn't seem so far apart—especially when it came to activism and advocacy. After all, I was pretty much protesting the same things and proclaiming the same fundamental human responsibility to shape this world from what it is to what it could be.

Liberal Protestantism—and Unitarian Universalism specifically—provided a home for my spirit. It was where I belonged. Except for one thing—that feeling down in my gut that ached from the very beginning, a fundamentally disquieting utopian sentiment within the liberal Protestant tradition that I still have not adequately resolved within myself. Namely: *We were so utterly and damnably sure of ourselves.*

In this new tribe that had adopted me, people were just so certain that they were right. They felt so sure that their interpretation of liberal theology or geopolitics was the correct one. So they moved in the world as though everyone else was just about to break through and come around to their perspective.

Given time, the good liberal church people seemed to think, everybody else would get on board, and together these enlightened souls would bring down those waters of justice and make sure peace rained down on the whole dang world like an ever-flowing stream. Perhaps we would start this inevitable process through a grand gesture of solidarity with all peoples—like planting a peace pole or flying the flag of the United Nations. Surely that would be a good beginning.

The kicker of it is that most of the time I didn't disagree with the utopian idealism of my self-assured fellow progressives. Much of what my colleagues and co-religionists asserted about the social, political, and theological world around us was not wrong—at least not when approached through the limited perceptions of my eager ear and receptive heart.

The challenging part was not the analysis or the visionary ideology; it was the utter certitude with which my fellow liberal religious leaders held those ideas. It was how entirely sure of themselves everyone seemed to be, and how little room there was to acknowledge their own limitations or the tragic dimension of time and history.

Somehow, this combination of self-assurance and moral clarity felt familiar, and not in a good way. Though I could not have stated it then, I knew that this confident projection of bright ideals was an aspect of my adopted tradition I would eventually have to come to terms with in order to serve the liberal church with authenticity, humility, and power.

Many years later, firmly ensconced in the trials and rewards of parish ministry, I write my sermons underneath a Peanuts cartoon I pasted on my office wall a decade ago. In it, Charlie Brown approaches Snoopy, who is perched atop his doghouse clacking away at his latest composition.

"I hear you're writing a book on theology," Charlie Brown says, "I hope you have a good title."

"I have the perfect title," replies Snoopy, in his perennial thought bubble. "Has It Ever Occurred to You That You Might Be Wrong?"

Snoopy's wisdom seems like an important corrective to the quasi-utopian idealism of the liberal church at the turn of the twenty-first century. We never considered that we might be wrong, or that our analysis may be incomplete. This basic stance of certitude and optimism was present enough in the theological academies, but more pervasive still in the liberal churches.

As I celebrated my quarter-century birthday from behind a pulpit, I looked for all the world like a starry-eyed cheerleader for the utopian progressive dream. But inside, I grappled with my congregants' tendencies to view themselves and our religious tradition as exceptional, the recipients of a legacy that prepared us to take our place in the arc of history as it bent ever-onward toward justice. I worried that my optimistic preaching furthered a false narrative—telling a fragile story about who we were that would fall apart into hopelessness the moment we honestly assessed the arc and found that its bent was neither clear nor uni-directional.

In those early years, I also encountered an unexamined yet oft-asserted optimism regarding human nature itself and a faithfulness to what we perceived as the generally upward trajectory of history.

All of this carried with it a tendency toward a kind of triumphalism in our understandings of time, history, and human potential. The story we told indicated that things were pointing in the right direction. And we—the mostly white, highly educated, and politically progressive religious liberals of our era—were surely the very ones to serve as our nation's moral compass, situating all others toward true north.

Progressive faith told a story of almost limitless possibility. It proclaimed human power when the orthodox traditions spoke of ontological brokenness. It made me believe in the world to come, a world that we could build with our own hands. I wanted to be a part of that progressive hopefulness. That vision moved me and salved my wounded places even as I quietly grappled with my role as a spokesperson and storyteller in such a tradition.

What I didn't know at the time was that this optimism comforted me partly because of my racial, ethnic, and socioeconomic location. I was a young white woman grappling with big theological questions. I wanted to believe that I, personally, was on the right side of history. The liberal church convinced me that, through activism, advocacy, and the righteous proclamation of a progressive vision, I could assure myself that I was.

It turns out that this viewpoint was framed, in part, to appeal to the same intellectual, educated, and cultivated souls who happened to populate the pews of the progressive church. The same souls whose defining identities and characteristics were not so different from my own.

As participants and leaders in mostly white middle-class institutions, our stories about progress focused almost entirely on the benevolent efforts of people who looked, spent, worked, and studied a whole lot like us. We proclaimed the inherent worth and dignity of every single human being, but we learned and served in institutions that put the dignity, power, possibility, and perspectives of some very self-assured white people at the center.

We were not the first, and perhaps will not be the last, generation of progressive religious leaders to do so.

For much of the past hundred years, even through wars, devastation, and the insidious persistence of systemic racism, modernist religious liberals in Eurocentric churches have preached about our near-unlimited capacity to fix just about everything that is broken. We have believed in ourselves so completely that the "good news" has become a good word about our own capacity to heal things, leaving little room for honest atonement or our own complicity in brokenness.

I have been claimed, convicted, and called by many of the ideals espoused within the liberal religious tradition. But I have never believed that thoughtful groups of good white people, united by grand ideals and graduate degrees, could propel those ideals into reality because of our faith in our own innate abilities.

In the latter years of my seminary education, I periodically imagined myself as a realist spy, infiltrating a network of compassionate and deeply engaged optimists. I posed as a perky twenty-something proto-preacher, but underneath I felt like a floating rain cloud, repeating the words "Yes but, yes but, yes but."

Yes, we believe that "we'll build a land where we bind up the broken,"[2] but what about human frailty? Yes, we believe that each person is born in inherent blessing, but what about sin? And yes, with Theodore Parker and Dr. King, we believe that "the arc of the moral universe is long, but it bends toward justice,"[3] but what about the ways in which our deep and unexamined privilege affects our view of history?

Why are we so quick to focus on the "bending toward justice" bit rather than honestly addressing the maddeningly long length of the arc—especially for people who live and struggle and lead at the margins of power?

In my early years among the liberal Protestants, I soon found that I was not in fact the only realist spy among the optimists. My fellow students and young preachers, many of them Gen Xers like myself, grappled with similar questions. We wondered just what it meant to uphold the bright blessings of the social gospel optimism that gave our movements power while still reconciling the truth of our lives and the world around us.

We wondered how to incorporate our own personal experiences of trauma and heartbreak with the almost-militant hymns of liberal optimism that rang from our lips in chapel services.

How would we preach this good news of expansive faith through the decades to come when we knew or suspected that those decades would bring with them devastation we could only begin to imagine? How would we live in the shadow of the dying progressive utopian dream while not allowing ourselves to give in to our generation's much-stated tendency toward cynicism or to the ever-present temptation to preach hollow truthiness in difficult times?

Preaching When Everything Is Falling Apart

My Gen X colleagues and I came into ministry in the immediate aftermath of 9-11, in the looming shadow of the war in Iraq. We rode the lashing waves of congregational life atop the rising tide of school shootings, over the cresting waters that burst through broken levees and onward, into the unflinching flood of honesty emerging from the Black Lives Matter movement.

Many of us found ourselves approaching the mid-points of our careers just in time for the post-election era of 2017, when the racial animus that had long served as the unspoken underpinning of American Democracy rose up and called itself by name. For most of our careers, people have been coming to church to dissect and respond to a series of tragic events whose meaning has not often been clear.

People also come to find hope amid these meaningful but continually evolving crises. The liberal church becomes a place to hold on to when everything else seems to swirl out of control, and those who fill our congregations on Sunday morning crave not only meaning but also ready access to comfort and assurance.

Thus, when the headlines break, which they do with dizzying speed, the people we serve in the liberal churches move quickly from wanting to know what it all means to wanting to know that it—whatever it is—will all be okay in the end. This rapid shift from meaning-making to assurance of comfort makes sense for many among the progressive worshippers we encounter. It is not a sin to hope for relief from the pressure of the headlines and the persistent drumbeat of bad news. It is not wrong to yearn for quick relief from existential and moral dis-ease.

However, the rapidity with which we move to meet this yearning for comfort and self-assurance is a conditioned response that sometimes arises from the racial and sociopolitical location of most worshippers in our pews. We are in a hurry to find comfort because we are used to living fundamentally comfortable lives.

Those who are accustomed to privilege consider it reasonable to expect comfort and assurance of their own fundamental decency. Much of their previous experience leads them to expect that their social, political, and religious life should be fundamentally okay on a deep existential level. Some are altogether unfamiliar with far-reaching ethical uncertainty, risk taking that stretches their personal safety, and persistent moral disquiet.

Most of the time, the people of the liberal church have not been asked to linger long in troubled waters. And yet, this rapid movement from meaning making to assurance of comfort—framed by white people and presented to white people—is jarring for those who live with no such expectation of safety or privilege. People at the center of the struggle and the margins of power do not often get the option to move on quickly. Sometimes the hopeful narratives that Eurocentric liberal churches create in order to make this quick-and-clean transition from tragedy to assurance strain credulity.

The unflappable self-assurance of privileged white people can be exhausting.

It is difficult to preach that all things shall grow into harmony with the divine when things seem to fall apart all around us. It is difficult to proclaim that this beautiful harmony will be created by the church itself when the church remains centered on the experiences and expectations of people who have spent far too long at the center of power.

Preachers of the liberal gospel are hard-pressed to be authentic in our liturgies and community practices while conforming to our traditions' utopian idealism regarding the inherent perfectibility of individuals and the upward trajectory of humankind. This is true even though many of the people we serve have come to expect exactly this kind of optimism on a Sunday morning.

In the years leading up to 1914, and then again in the decades following the Second World War, the modernist progressive utopian dream taught that the ideals we hold dear can be achieved through the steady advance of moral cultivation, a dedication to learning, and church-based community action. Protestant progressives have been preaching this utopian vision for generations. That utopia, like so many others before it, is all but dead, and it is time that we admit it. It is also time for us to reconstruct something more honest, and arguably more powerful, from those ashes.

Today, the idea of idealism is not enough. Casual optimism rings hollow, and triumphal, self-assured liturgies leave our broken hearts still yearning for the chance to sing together in a minor key. The people we serve yearn for that too, for an honest word and an opportunity to hold our shared grief and deep personal brokenness together in community on a Sunday morning. We cannot offer the cheap grace of eventual societal perfection in times of systemic desolation, and we cannot sell one another on the idea that it's all going to be just fine in the end.

The liberal church is being called to a new way of being, a less self-assured but equally faithful approach to living and serving in these times. Daniel Berrigan, one of the late great radicals of my liberal Catholic heritage, once said, "How [do we] build a life worthy of human beings in the darkness? We are called to grow new organs, by new conditions of life and death. New ways of perceiving, of living in the world, new ways of moving over, to give room for others to live at our side."[4]

This project arises from my own discomfort at the certitude of the good liberal people I have come to love, to lead, and to serve alongside. It is also inspired by the faithfulness and courage many in my own Unitarian Universalist tradition are currently bringing to the work of dismantling of white supremacy and decentering whiteness in our institutions.

This effort to build a new way of worshipping and proclaiming hope in the liberal church does not depend on triumphal self-assurance. It is fueled daily by the resilience, truth telling, and humble courage of the people who weep and laugh alongside me during daily parish life.

The people I serve tell the truth. There is a reason I can never seem to locate any tissue boxes in my office—those tissue boxes move all around the spaces we have made sacred, flowing as freely as the tears. As a minister, the invitation offered to me, day after day, week after week, is to somehow articulate the full truth of my people's deep human experience and deeper human longing, all while pointing us forward with both hope and commitment.

My abiding love for the progressive church stands in creative tension against the fundamental critiques of this book—liberal optimism, attachment to respectability, the centering of whiteness, and a progressivist view of history. These critiques apply to the congregation and the denomination in which I serve as acutely as anywhere else in the world of progressive religion. And yet these critiques cannot arise from less generous a sentiment than love for the people I serve—a love that would be greatly diminished if I remained too cautious or too comfortable to offer honest critique of the broader liberal religious culture that holds us all.

After all, church is church is church is church. Much of what we struggle with in my own tradition, we struggle with together across the Protestant spectrum and beyond.

And though many of the resources in this text are drawn from my own Unitarian Universalist tradition, I hope these pages will illustrate that mine are not the only people in the liberal church who are a little too sure of themselves. We also aren't the only people with a persistent tendency to skip right on to the triumph of Easter while barely nodding our heads at the horror of Good Friday, nor are we by any means the primary religious and institutional home for the performance of white-centered respectability.

Likewise, when it comes to excessive confidence in our own capacity, attachment to middle-class comfort, and faith in the upward trajectory of history, Unitarian Universalists do not have a corner on the market.

I also know that this discomfort with a fundamentally optimistic progressivism is not at all unique to me, nor even to my fellow cynical—yet soul-searching—denizens of Generation X. Generations before us have ached to tell the truth, while simultaneously proclaiming a propulsive and inspirational hope. Others before us, both within and outside of the liberal Protestant tradition, have pointed out the same flaws in our triumphal progressive imaginings.

This project is not unique, in either conception or design. It's merely an effort to communicate a few things that so many of us on the left-leaning side of the religious spectrum have been thinking lately and weeping over from time to time. It's born of a desire to remain faithful to the hope and power of the ones who went before us in liberal religion, while also not hiding behind their once-shiny ideas of progressive optimism—especially the idea that each congregation of worshippers within the Eurocentric liberal church could personally build a land where we bind up the broken and set free all the captives whose imprisonment we ourselves have profited from.

And so, as we move forward from this situation, we all must begin where we are. We can't borrow anybody else's story. We can't wear another's oppression or experience like a brand-new suit, tags still on, that we might just return later in the day. We can only tell our own stories with honesty while forthrightly putting ourselves in proximity to the stories, the tragedies, the triumphs, and the living and dying utopian dreams of those fellow travelers we hold dear.

To begin at the beginning, for me, is to go home again to the dead utopias of my personal history and communal heritage. The progressive utopian experiments that are part of my hometown history crumbled long before I lived. And the privileged Eurocentric ideals of my chosen religious tradition are crumbling all around us. Taken together, they pervade each corner of my life and ministry.

The story can't be told without starting right there—at home. Back in the shadow of two dead utopias.

One

The Shadow of the Dead Utopias

> Here it is . . . in the heart of the United States and almost in the centre of its unequalled internal navigation, that Power which directs and governs the universe and every action of man, has arranged . . . to permit me to commence a new empire of peace and good will to men, founded on other principles and leading to other practices than those of present or past, and which principles, in due season, and in the allotted time, will lead to that state of virtue, intelligence, enjoyment and happiness which has been foretold by the sages of past.
> —Robert Owen[5]

My parents' little ranch house sits in a patch of cornfield not far from New Harmony, Indiana, the site of two of America's once-heralded and later-lamented attempts at utopian communal living. Some say that American socialism itself was born in my conservative and buttoned-up home county—as was the first kindergarten in the United States, the first public school in the state, and the biggest embarrassment in the entire history of American secular idealism.

I am a Hoosier by birth, though not even people from Indiana seem to know exactly what that means. In most settings, saying you're from Indiana is basically just a generic way of calling yourself a Midwesterner. Saying you are from *southern* Indiana specifically is a way of indicating that you are more than just a little bit country. If there is a cosmopolitan part of Indiana, we are not it.

I grew up in flat and fertile river land. There is corn there, a whole lot of it. And industrial decline. And methamphetamine addiction. And racism. And locally grown watermelons. And a great lot of fundamentally decent people. And patriarchy. And small-town charm. There is all of that.

And, at least in the rural corner of the state from which I sprouted, there are also the ideological and archeological remains of two separate waves of nineteenth-century travelers from distant shores who believed they could come out to these vast tracts of river-fed "wilderness" and build a whole new world.

Of course, the wilderness in which they settled was not a wilderness at all, but land important enough in the complex societies of the Hopewell and Oto Sioux that the remnants of their burial mounds are still evident within the perimeter of the town's historic walled cemetery. The mounds roll gently beside the unmarked graves of the early utopians, evidence of habitation, cultivation, and prosperity that were there long before Europeans came to plant their dreams of a whole new world.

By 1804, the Treaty of Vincennes had enabled white settlers to claim land throughout the Indiana territory bordered by the Buffalo Trace in the north, the Ohio River on the south, and the Wabash River to the west. By the time the utopians came, the removal of native peoples had created the illusion of a vast unspoiled pastoral paradise awaiting settlement by a willing European buyer.

The first willing buyers were from a group of pietist pilgrims who immigrated to the United States after splitting from the German Lutheran church in 1785 and being banned from gathering together or joining in public prayer.

Calling themselves the Harmonie society, these bonnet-and-beard-sporting German-speaking separatists attempted communal living in rural Pennsylvania before eventually purchasing significant Hoosier acreage along a fertile bend in the Wabash River in 1814.

The Harmonists, or "Rappites" as today's locals tend to call them with a note of gentle disdain, were more properly millenarian than utopian. Numbering about five hundred in total, they were led by a commanding, square-shouldered, and disarmingly charismatic preacher named George Rapp. Not long after arriving in the southern Indiana river bottoms, they had laid out an orderly grid of five city blocks and were hard at work creating a perfectly comfortable society in which to wait out the end of the world.

This seems like odd behavior, in retrospect. When viewed from a twenty-first-century lens, it's all cultish and strange to follow the commands of some black-hatted preacher, plant your flag on a muddy riverbank, and wait for the end times in the middle of nowhere. And yet, history shows that this sort of end-time expectation and can-do utopian social imagination was not such a strange choice back in those days. Everybody was doing it.

Mine are not the only dead utopias. There were no less than 130 separate attempts to set up utopian communities in the United States during the nineteenth century; 130 separate efforts to create heaven on earth, each based on different communal assumptions, theological convictions, and degrees of commitment to various social reforms.

There were utopian teetotalers and utopian libertines, utopian renunciants of the pleasures of the flesh and utopian free-lovers bent on reclaiming every single pleasure flesh had to offer. There were utopian spiritualists who labored in the fields of another world and utopian plain-livers who planted beans in the most perfectly ordered rows that this world has ever seen before or since. There were utopian women's rights advocates jaunting around the fruit trees in scandalous pantaloons and utopian communal societies overseen by male authority figures who tended to see women as breeding stock in a larger plan of supposedly benevolent eugenics.

There was also a smattering of semi-secular utopian socialist reformers, many of whom found themselves in uneasy conversations with the various varieties of utopian reincarnations of Christ.

Reflecting on the fervor among his own progressive circle of Boston intellectuals, Ralph Waldo Emerson once wrote to a friend overseas that, "We are all a little wild here with numerous projects of social reform. Not a reading man but has a draft of a new community in his waistcoat pocket."[6]

Everywhere they went, the utopians, end-timers, reformers, and reincarnations of Christ left their marks on the landscape and the people they interacted with, nowhere more dramatically than the place where I grew up.

There in the fertile flatlands of Harmonie, the Rappites were so convinced of the end times that they decided to sharply curtail their own reproduction as much as possible. From a generational perspective, that choice didn't work out so well, either for them or for the more famous Shakers, who went all in and managed to ban sex altogether among the brethren of their whole new world.

Like other utopians, the Rappites had some troubling inconsistencies. They generally practiced celibacy and lived in modestly undifferentiated dwellings, even though their leader had his conspicuously large family installed in a big brick mansion in the middle of town. They awaited the end times, yet contributed robustly to the capitalist economy of the pre–Civil War era. They discouraged the vice of alcohol, yet carried on a widely successful commercial enterprise through the vineyards they planted just outside of town. They proclaimed that the dispensing of justice rested squarely in the hands of God, but fortified a massive stone granary that doubled as a nearly impregnable redoubt, just in case they had to take justice into their own hands.

Like the Shakers, they too believed that American religion was hopelessly corrupt and that a pure form of human society could be created here in the terrestrial plane while waiting out the time before the impending end. The problem was, the end just didn't come fast enough.

After carving their functional society from the wilderness, the Rappites quickly figured out that waiting for the end of the world in the middle of nowhere while shipping their commercial products downriver to New Orleans and out to markets in the east was really damn expensive.

So, in 1824, the Harmonie Society sold their utopia. They got back on their riverboats and headed back out to Pennsylvania to wait for the end of the world in a more economically feasible fashion. They continued to hold their ideals but maintained their place in the economic structure in which they were resoundingly successful participants.

So much for the first perfect society in my old stomping grounds.

As a twenty-first-century progressive, I am all bound up in a historical-critical approach to scripture that reads the various expressions of end-times eschatology within the Christian tradition as an artifact of first-century Jewish oppression under the thumb of the Roman Empire.

As such, I can easily hold the Rappites and their world's end expectation of imminent doom at arm's length. The problems they faced in their effort to build a perfect society are, for the most part, not really my problems. The horizon of possibilities they waited for is not the one I'm seeking, and the edifice of their whole new world, while worthy of study and consideration, was not built on the same foundation as the progressive utopian ideals that seem to crumble all around me now in the twenty-first-century liberal church.

Beyond a certain heartbreaking complicity, present in both their time and our own, between successful business ventures and larger economic systems that profit from land theft, domination, and white supremacy, the legacy of their communal failure is one of intellectual curiosity for me more than personal or contemporary significance.

The same convenient distance doesn't really apply to the second failed utopia in my hometown. In ways I will probably always be grappling with, the second dead utopia feels way too familiar.

The New Moral World

The Harmonists were followed directly by what may have been the most celebrated utopian experiment in the history of secular America. It became a powerful testament to one man's abiding faith in himself and in a nation's eager willingness to believe that heaven on earth was imminently possible on purely human terms through a kind of benevolent social engineering.

Following the utilitarian ideals that framed the greatest good for the greatest number of people, this new New Harmony experiment would reach for nothing less grand than the full and complete happiness of all the people, all the time, everywhere.

The founder not only believed that this all-encompassing good society was imminently possible, but also that it was replicable across the whole sweep of human culture. He truly believed that the only thing the world was waiting for was one single artfully executed example. The perfect society would start in one place and circle outward to claim not just the town of New Harmony but the entire nation and the entire world.

The building of a whole new world would take some doing, these new utopians knew. There would be difficult decisions. Yet, the denizens of this second utopia argued, all things were possible in the American frontier, especially if we can get all of that pesky stuff like culture, religion, and family loyalty out of the way first. They believed those were just obstacles and details that shielded the greater view of a higher unified vision for all people.

There is a big, clumsy-looking painting hanging in the library in New Harmony today; it depicts the transition from one failed Utopia to another—from pietistic religious millenarianism to self-assured socially progressive utopian idealism.

The painting shows a seated George Rapp, in his severe outfit and Santa beard, signing over the deed to the whole town lock stock and barrel to his successor—a well-dressed, frock-coated Scottish philanthropist named Robert Owen. While the two in fact never met in person, the transaction depicted in that awkward painting was real enough. Owen paid $125,000 for the town and took personal possession of the land well before he had quite worked out who exactly would be invited to join him in the much-feted creation of what he called the New Moral World.

When Robert Owen took possession of the town that would become New Harmony, he was a wealthy man. Like the Rappites before him, he fully participated in the commerce of his era. No one could plunk down that much cash without succeeding in the emerging industrial economy, and Owen had done awfully well for himself—impressive when you consider that he did so while forging a path of industrial and social reform that briefly made him one of the most famous men in all of Europe.

Born to no particular wealth in Wales just before the American Revolution, Owen was a bookish young student who read everything he could get his hands on about classical Western philosophy and economic theory. As a young man, he managed to gain a toehold in the textile industry by purchasing a few of his own looms and hiring a handful of employees.

Owen had good timing. When he got on board with the practice of importing mass quantities of slave-tended cotton from the Southern American states and turning it into inexpensive linen, there was a great deal of money to be made. Before long, he was the owner and operator of a massive textile mill in New Lanark, Scotland. After reading utilitarian philosophy and studying Plato for most of his young life, this privileged, intelligent, and educated man finally had the chance to combine his theoretical life of study with his power and influence over one small corner of the industrial economy.

When Owen purchased his mill in Scotland, it was operated largely by hundreds of child laborers who worked up to sixteen hours a day and began their employment as young as five years old. He saw these children, their parents, and the entire economy of the mill itself as a vast project of reform. To him, the enterprise was grand and full of possibility. The people themselves were both pitiable and full of potential.

Owen wanted to lessen the suffering of the children at the New Lanark mill. He also believed that they and their parents were entirely in his care and that his primary role in relationship to them was to serve as the benevolent overseer of their well-being. Whether they chose to participate in this arrangement or not, the workers in New Lanark found themselves in his hands.

To him, the poor children of the industrial economy were a kind of malleable clay that could be shaped through early and kind-hearted intervention into the model citizens that could ultimately populate a model society. That early intervention into the shaping of their character and the consequent reshaping of society itself was to be

Owen's supreme task in the world. Children, he once said, were "passive and wonderfully contrived compounds."[7] Like the supposedly unbroken soil of a wilderness utopia, they were merely waiting for someone just like him to come and shape them into glorious, refulgent flowers of moral men and women.

Owen's primary philosophy was an adaptation of John Locke's idea of human nature as a "tabula rasa," or blank slate. Nature had nothing to do with the formation of character, Owen believed. The circumstance of the society into which human beings were born shaped them utterly. Therefore, he believed, it was morally obligatory for persons of high character and capacity—such as himself—to shape the social context in which children and families were brought up. As he put it, with the bold all-caps style characteristic of his rather intense persona, "It is of all truths the most important, that the character of man is formed FOR—not BY—himself."[8]

That is to say, people are not self-determined creatures. They are determined utterly and completely by their surroundings.

Theologically, this was something of a radical concept at the time. Much religious debate hinged upon the innate good or evil of the human creature, mediated through the workings of a benevolent or demanding God. He was pushing the envelope, but Owen's fellow progressives and social reformers tended to meet this ideology with wary but willing appreciation.

Ralph Waldo Emerson once included thoughts on the great reformer in a letter to his brother when he said, "I am no fanatic disciple of Mr. Owen; I nourish no predilection for the exploded experiments of New Harmony. . . . Yet I must venture on the repetition of an ancient truism that every man's character depends in great part upon the scope & occasions that have been afforded him for its development."[9]

Indeed, the way society forms us and the impact of our surroundings have everything to do with who we become as participants in community life and moral agents in the world. This is as true today as it was in the early industrial age. Circumstance contributes to the accessibility of opportunity, and the soil in which a flower is planted has a direct and immediate impact on the potential beauty of the eventual bloom.

It is also worth noting that, at least in the New Lanark cotton mill, the surroundings of every single human being were largely determined by Robert Owen himself. The soil in which each human flower was planted was managed, tended, controlled, and owned by a rich white man who held the power to offer or to deny a great many things.

Owen's reforms at the mill were far-reaching, impactful, and controversial. Almost immediately, he cut two hours off the nearly interminable work day without docking pay. He raised the age of hire and opened the first kindergarten outside of Germany, specifically for the families of his workers. With an experiential and practical pedagogy not unlike modern Montessori education, his factory school taught the sciences, history, and geography at a time when most children of the British laboring class were mired in illiteracy.

Salaries at his looms were higher than the norm, the company store sold everything at cost, and workers were reported by the many visitors who came through the mill to be in a nearly unified state of ease and gratification. Through all of this, Owen loudly and publicly declared that there was no ontological difference between himself and his workers and that his own success was purely a product of circumstance, just as their success could be ensured through the proper and fully embraced implementation of his reforms.

By the time his reforms were fully realized in New Lanark, the workers who enjoyed higher pay and free education also had the privacy of their homes impinged upon by unannounced searches and the integrity of their bodies violated through random pat-downs. In addition, the quality of their work was continually overseen with the same benevolent paternalism that characterized all of Owen's interactions with the very people he sought to uplift.

He even went so far as to install strange wooden blocks above the workstations of his employees. On these blocks, notes on the employee's character and performance would be displayed for all

passers-by to praise or otherwise comment upon. Called "silent mon-
itors," they were painted in four different colors to signify four different qualitative measures of performance. Predictably enough, white
signified excellence of character. Black signified the opposite. All was
recorded. Over all of it was Owen himself, managing his project of
industrial reform with utmost attention while continuing to dream
of a whole new world.

Owen's model factory was just the beginning. It served as a test-
ing ground for his ideals of a model society and whetted his appetite
for a larger visionary experiment altogether—a perfect order of communal living, built from the ground up on utopian principles of pure
human potential.

His perfect society would include common ownership of goods
and property, opportunities for educational advancement, and the
broad encouragement of scientific inquiry. The social conventions of
religion, class distinctions, and marriage that held back the development of the Old World would be stripped away entirely. Somewhere
in the American frontier, he was certain he would find the starting
point from which his vision might expand to capture the hearts of—
literally—all the people in the entire world.

And so, when a patch of fertile flatland came open in southern
Indiana, with an empty little town already there, Owen didn't hes-
itate to pack up his interests, pocket a letter of introduction to the
president of the United States himself, and set out to build the New
Moral World in what would eventually become my own backyard.

The transaction between the Harmonists and the great reformer did in fact happen, though not in quite the way the awkward
painting shows. And once he cut that great big check with all the
self-assurance and horn-tooting celebration that came along with it,
Robert Owen set out to build this model society on Hoosier soil.

While he did not attend much at all to the town's eventual working populace, Owen began gathering colleagues and friends around
him who shared his ideology, moral sentiment, and personal capacity
to affect change. They were like-minded, progressive, educated, and
profoundly self-assured.

Owen was certain that his ideals were true and that his vision would become a vastly accepted new reality. He was also certain that the expertly curated batch of super-enlightened people whom he would personally gather together in New Harmony would be the beginning of a whole new world. As Emerson said, Owen "had not the least doubt that he had hit on a right and perfect socialism, or that all mankind would adopt it."[10]

The Boatload of Knowledge

Owen was so convinced—and so convincing—that by the time his steamship landed in New York, he had converted a number of his shipmates. Throughout his journey to New Harmony to take possession of the town, he met with former presidents and current power players. Once the deal with the Rappites was completed, Owen left his son in charge of the two thousand acres he had bought and headed back to the East Coast to generate interest and financial support from the cultivated intellectuals he believed were essential to the success of his experiment.

Chief among those fellow idealists was a world-famous geologist and educational reformer named William Maclure. Maclure held no less shiny a title than President of the Academy of Natural Sciences of Philadelphia, and the company he kept was rarefied indeed. Like Owen, he believed that truly universal education was the key to advancement of the laboring classes. Unlike Owen, he focused on education to the exclusion of many of the more abstract or high-vaunted expectations inherent in the new experiment. At least in the beginning, they were a match made in their own mutual conception of a populist heaven.

Working their progressive and forward-thinking networks of colleagues and acquaintances, these two gentlemen managed to convince a group of astonishingly well-connected East Coast intellectuals to board an eighty-five-foot flatboat in Pittsburgh and float down the Ohio River to Indiana in a coterie that they had the audacity to call the "Boatload of Knowledge."

It was said that the journey of the Boatload of Knowledge constituted one of the single most significant intellectual migrations in American history. Owen himself declared that it held "more learning than ever was contained before on a boat,"[11] and he placed his great hope for the future of the perfect society on the cultivating force embodied by these creative and scientific powerhouses.

The Boatload of Knowledge was to be the seed of his new society. As such, it was replete with poets and geologists, cartographers, and educational reformers. There were more advanced degrees held by its denizens than by the entire populace of the county in which they set out to make their home.

It was an impressive assortment to say the least, and yet there were some notable absences. Most importantly, there was nary a single farmer, tradesperson, or laborer among their lot. The debates on moral philosophy, Byronic poetry, and social welfare that raged on that boat must have been heady, but tangible conversations about how to grow food and cut firewood in this new Eden of theirs perhaps were not so well-informed.

New York society and Philadelphia's great universities toasted the Boatload of Knowledge at their departure. People lined the waterways, waving handkerchiefs to bid them luck as they progressed toward this ultimate destination of a new Eden on the Wabash River. As they set out, all was optimism, brightness, possibility, and hope.

And so, bent on probing all the mysteries of the universe, the Boatload of Knowledge disembarked that winter of 1826 on the selfsame muddy riverfront embankment where my more daring high school friends parked their cars for late-night assignations more than a century and a half later.

They made their way toward what they hoped would become a Village of Unity and Mutual Cooperation, down a muddy path that would eventually be home to the now-shuttered neighborhood bar where my big sister may or may not have once set off a series of cherry bombs in the women's restroom.

We know that the Boatload of Knowledge disembarked in Mt. Vernon, Indiana, and eventually made their way to the small, neatly laid out town Owen had purchased from the Rappites in the all-inclusive way one may now purchase a vacation home in the Poconos. Everything was included, except the people.

That bit, it turned out, posed something of a problem. Beyond the great minds on the Boatload of Knowledge, Owen had not paid careful attention to who came to join in the collective experiment of the New Moral World. He had essentially put out an ad indicating that anyone who wanted to build a new world was welcome to come on out, and the people who had arrived in New Harmony in the months between Owen's purchase and the Boatload's arrival were a rather motley crew.

Those who arrived to populate the community of cooperation ranged from true believers to roustabouts. They came from all over the country in one of the most ideologically diverse assemblages to be found in the entire Western Hemisphere. All were welcome—except "persons of color." I guess the perfect society just didn't include anybody who wasn't white. The Owenite reformers paid no attention to the racial dynamics of society at large—even though most of the town's progressive luminaries professed broad and nonspecific abolitionist sympathies, and even though Owen's fortune was made in direct complicity with the slave structure of the American cotton industry.

And so, the supposedly classless and universalized populace of New Harmony was made up largely from two distinctly polarized groups of white people—the urban intellectuals who were drawn to the ideals of Owen's philosophy and the unskilled laborers who arrived in hope of a steady job and a warm bed to sleep in. Notably, there were few skilled laborers, artisans, and established area farmers.

Robert Dale Owen, the son of the reformer and a prominent civic leader himself, once described the mixed bag tossed together in New Harmony as a "heterogeneous collection of radicals, enthusiastic devotees to principle, honest latitudinarians and lazy theorists, with a sprinkling of unprincipled sharpers thrown in."[12]

While that scene sounds like a lot of fun, it does not necessarily have the makings of a successful communal economy.

In time, some among those celebrated thinkers would sow seeds that grew into significant intellectual and social movements around the country. Today, the town of New Harmony has too small and too elderly a population to support its own public school, but it was there that America's public school movement gained its first ideological support. Early childhood education was pioneered in that little village. Even after the economics of the New Harmony experiment fell apart, William Maclure continued to use the town as the home base for his ongoing and enormously successful efforts to establish free public education throughout the country.

Today, the Working Men's Institute, also founded by William Maclure, still stands as a one of the earliest lending libraries in the United States. Even now, it carries on its original mission of bridging the information gap between the wealthy and the poor. The building erected to house that institute—by a grateful alumnus of the Owenite education system—still graces the center of town after 180 years of continuous operation.

To this day, local townies like me go to the museum housed above that library to leer at an eight-legged calf, preserved through taxidermy, that was born on a nearby farm sometime around 1900. We also slide open drawers of shells and stones collected by the Boatload's scientists almost two hundred years ago, some of which are still being actively catalogued and preserved by universities today.

And yet, for all the possibilities and ideals that came with them on that boat up the river, those progressive intellectuals still had a great deal to learn. As the Boatload itself and the existing population of the town attested, they didn't know a whole hell of a lot about farming. This posed something of a challenge in the fertile floodplain of the Wabash River.

While every person was expected to bend their back at manual labor, the wealthier among the townspeople could effectively buy their way out of the really difficult stuff. Within just a few months the residents were reduced to purchasing foodstuffs from local farmers outside of the communal economy, all while Father Rapp's old plowshares sat unused in his perfectly tidy abandoned barns.

That was the primary tension in the New Harmony experiment—the ideals and the realities just didn't align. The utopians, despite their progressive idealism, still had a hard time relating meaningfully to the economically marginalized laborers who joined them in the New Moral World. Meanwhile, the skilled workers and artisans required to support a functioning rural economic system were increasingly hesitant to sign themselves over to so paternalistic and economically shaky an enterprise. Robert Owen, convinced that the full flowering of his society could only happen when all property was held in common, still found himself holding roles of bank, landlord, and overseer.

After an initial attempt at a communal economy failed, the people worked the land, but Owen owned it. Owning it turned out to be an increasingly economically dubious proposition, as it was soon apparent that the whole thing was going under fast. Caught up in a lack of planning, the shaky finances of their visionary leader himself, and the fact that the most useful and productive members of the society were increasingly disillusioned by the impracticability of it all, the experiment spiraled quickly into moral compromise and ultimate dissolution.

In a relatively short time, the ideals—so clean and bright in the abstract—came crashing into the realities, which were muddled and tainted by capitalistic necessities. The Boatload and their benevolent friends couldn't afford to hold common property anymore. What began as a model of socialist secular idealism became just a small Midwestern town with a significant number of creative, smart people living on their privately owned property.

That's basically what New Harmony is today. It's a small Midwestern town with many retirees, some cute historic buildings, and higher-than-average populations of feminist theorists, avant-garde spiritual seekers, modernist gallery owners, and artisanal soap makers.

In a great many ways, this ultimate devolution from high-vaunted utopian socialist ideals to a quaint, capitalistic artist's haven has had positive results for the people who live there. I love it there. In fact, it is exactly the kind of artistic, creative, spiritually progressive, and mostly white environment in which I and other religious liberals like me tend to feel most at home. *Let that sink in for a minute.*

Literal and Ideological Remains of Dead Utopias

We started this whole story with my admission that I grew up in the shadow of dead utopias. As a liberal religious leader, I work, lead, and follow within the context of a dying modernist progressive vision. The fundamentally paternalistic dead utopia of my personal history surely informs my ongoing discomfort with the progressive utopian idealism evidenced in liberal religion. There was a reason all that bloviating self-assurance I experienced in my early years among the liberal Protestants seemed familiar.

I have found a home for my spirit in spiritually progressive and idealistic liberal religion. And here is the important linkage—underneath it all, the creative, artistic, and mostly white environment of liberal Protestantism in the twenty-first century *looks and feels very much like the compromised capitalistic remnants of the dead utopia in which I was raised.*

I traded one Eurocentric, semi-enlightened liberal sphere of do-gooder optimism for another. I upgraded from the literal remnants of one dead utopia to the ideological remnants of another. And it is within those ideological remnants of the compromised, Eurocentric, do-gooder modernist utopia of liberal Protestant religion that I frankly continue to feel most at home.

There is a reason that I, a white woman with a good liberal arts education, an appreciation for a finely crafted latte, and a carefully inculcated social conscience, feel at home in progressive Protestantism today. Liberal churches in the twenty-first century, and Unitarian Universalist churches in particular, are predominantly framed for people like me, by people like me, with assumptions, categorizations, and limitations of perception much like my own. The compromises we reach when our own ideals crumble are compromises that favor the comfort and satisfaction of educated, refined, and privileged people.

The quaint and artistic capitalist compromise that New Harmony eventually evolved into remains the perfect stomping grounds for do-gooder optimists like me. Yet, I cannot escape the fact that the narrowly framed and socially dislocated assumptions of those on the Boatload of Knowledge are ideologically related to the progressive triumphalism in evidence throughout the liberal church today.

If the eschatology of the Rappite end times is easy to hold at arm's length, the same cannot be said of the professed human perfectibility and patronizing projects of reform that characterized the Owenite social experiment.

The Bible-thumping blood atonements of American fundamentalism may be easy for me to stand firmly against while they continue to be co-opted by nativist and isolationist forces on the political right. But the same cannot be said for the lukewarm, altogether bloodless professions of friendship, tolerance, and universal lovey-dovey benevolence often expressed in Sunday mornings in mainline Protestant churches.

This safe distance from the actual experiences and circumstances of suffering is attainable only in a state of privilege. And it is every bit as present in the liberal church today as it has been in American reformist traditions for generations.

The forces that conspired to compromise Robert Owen's bold vision of shared property, intellectual advancement, and educational reform all the way back in 1827 are the very forces that hinder the courageous and authentic development of liberal religious communities today. Those forces include the following:

- A profound, sometimes naive faith in the upward trajectory of history, guided by an equally profound and equally naive faith in humanity's capacity to affect that upward trajectory of change.
- This faith in human capacity, while abstractly universalist in character, is mostly circumscribed around a very specific set of people—usually a small circle of uniformly elite, largely male, and overwhelmingly white intellectuals—who personally construct a broadly stated vision that lays claim to their ultimate loyalty.

- A habit of parachuting in from out of town or out of context on projects of benevolent paternalism not grounded in authentic relationship to the communities in which such reforms are planted.
- An inability or persistent refusal on the part of the privileged reformers to place themselves within their social location or to acknowledge and atone for the ways in which they have benefitted from the oppression of others.

What is the cost of these shared corrupting forces? What do they do to the good progressive reformers, both in ages past and every single day in the lived experience of the present? For the secular utopians in the New Harmony experiment, the cost was—at the very least—the loss of their reformist dream. For Robert Owen, it was the sinking of a whole bunch of money and a significant portion of his reputation into something that was never destined to work.

More importantly, the cost of these corrupting forces was also paid in the lives and livelihoods of native peoples, slaves, immigrant laborers, and middle-class workers. Utopia was built on stolen land, with money earned from willing participation in a slave society. Neither the unskilled immigrant laborers who came in search of a better life nor the local people who first tended the land benefitted much from the arrival of these grand idealists.

In the end, Owen was more loyal to his own broadly stated ideals than he was to the people who sacrificed in service of those ideals, and the progressive reform project he undertook had more to do with his own vision than it did with the people who came together to live within the shelter of his supposed benevolence.

His dead utopia was a grandly stated scheme. Its character was a bit wacky and the pace of its failure a bit extreme. Yet in many ways, it was not so different from the self-assured, often paternalistic, and disconnected Eurocentric progressive religion in which so many of us live and serve today.

Where the great reformers of a former age failed, so do we. Where they sinned in the hubris of their vision, so do we. And where the elites among them refused to push their ideals far enough feel the pinch of discomfort, so do we as religious liberals continue to refuse the discomfort of the anti-oppressive vision that calls us forward.

After all, the remnants of a dead utopia—either a literal or an ideological one—aren't so bad a place for privileged white people to live in. There are art galleries. And artisanal soap. And book clubs. And other like-minded, privileged, white people. Isn't that enough?

Those Who Labor in the Vineyards

I came to a liberal Protestant tradition mostly because the people there welcomed me with a broad and loving grace, powerful enough to knock me to my knees in gratitude. I also came because the theological underpinnings of a loving, nonpersonified god; a broadly defined system of human freedom; and a liturgically grounded practice of communal responsibility felt not only comforting and homey, but true.

I suspect some part of me also came to the liberal Protestant tradition because it was a way of moving up in the world, a means of finally counting myself as a passenger on the Boatload of Knowledge.

I hitched myself to a tradition grounded in the same liberal optimism, privileged intellectualism, and visionary capacity carried on the Boatload of Knowledge. I could imagine myself there, debating philosophy on the Wabash River instead of coming to terms with another part of who I also am—one of the local townies who worked in service to the high-minded guests and cleaned up the messes they made as they packed up and left town.

My own personal genealogy is not very well developed. Though my dad has some grave rubbings and my uncle has followed some leads, we don't really know when many of my ancestors made it to the fertile flatlands of southern Indiana or why they made their home there.

I do know that my people didn't get feted by scions of Philadelphia society when they showed up in Posey County, Indiana. There were no graduate degrees in the lot, which included farmers, a few loggers, and one mean Baptist lady preacher. On one side of my family tree, traced through my grandmother, my ancestors in the region were essentially German and Irish sharecroppers. They were poor immigrant people, newly endowed with the made-up identity of working class American "whiteness." They were minimally educated tenant farmers who worked land owned by others.

If I am literally descended from the people who participated in New Harmony's utopia, my heritage does not lie with the Boston Brahmins and Philadelphia intellectuals who parachuted in to benevolently oversee the project of social reform. Nor does it lie with the First Nations peoples who dotted that landscape with low-rising mounds or the mind-boggling number of enslaved Africans whose cotton filled Owen's coffers. Rather, my heritage lies with the laborers who worked to plant the vineyards of utopia, even though the ideals of that perfect society failed to include them in its embrace.

As a kid, I took field trips to the dead utopias. I eagerly watched demonstrations of butter churning and rope making that took place while the costumed interpreters told me about the imminent end of the world in Rappite theology. I witnessed history as I ran my fingers over the still-besmeared printing press of the Owenite socialist reformers.

As a teenager, I cleaned the hotel rooms and did the dishes of the labyrinth walkers, spiritual searchers, poets-in-residence, and aging hippies who came to pay homage to the ideals of a former age. On my lunch breaks, I walked the pathways laid out by those who came to my homeland to lay straight the way of the Lord.

As a young adult in my early twenties, I too followed the Lord's path, though in a manner those Harmonist ancestors would not have perceived as anything akin to the straight and narrow.

Expanding the Vision of the Utopian Dream

In the life of a Unitarian Universalist seminary student, there are thinkers and writers whose influence one cannot ignore. Even in the digital age, any worthy seminary experience includes a few encounters with fragile paper in dusty libraries that change your life. Even still, there are books you remember picking up for the very first time.

It was during those heady days in seminary that I was first introduced to James Luther Adams, a twentieth-century liberal theologian who once taught at my own seminary in Chicago. Adams's contemporaries told a story that he used to retire to his room for a daily mid-day cat-nap, to watch soap operas just like my grandma used to do. I have always hoped that anecdote is true.

Whenever his stories weren't on TV, Adams spent his time in the mid- to late-twentieth century delivering deeply felt and biting critiques of the social location, historic triumphalism, and naive optimism of the Unitarian tradition. His thinking has shaped me profoundly, so his work appears all over the pages that stretch out before us. So do the ideas and ideals expressed by liberal religious luminaries like William Ellery Channing, Hosea Ballou, and the twentieth-century modernists of Protestant progressivism, whose pulpits are still venerated like shrines in their denominational contexts.

More importantly, we will look at the ways in which the optimistic misconceptions and broad lack of perception that brought down the secular utopia in my hometown have also been at work in the American liberal tradition at large.

If the Owenite reformers in my hometown couldn't expand the vision of utopia to include my own laboring-class ancestors, can my own progressive brethren do a little bit better in our time?

What will it take for the utopian dreamers in today's liberal churches to actually listen to the voices we are accustomed to bellowing over? Perhaps we can be more authentic and relationally grounded than those limited visionaries who blazed a path across my hometown long before I was born.

I serve a liberal Unitarian Universalist church full of people with "open minds, loving hearts, and helping hands." I love that church, and I love these people. I love the earnestness of their intent and the commitment that undergirds every single one of their efforts.

I also know that I can serve as their minister partly because—like the passengers on the Boatload of Knowledge—I can perform my intelligence and debate natural philosophy all day long. Like those earlier reformers, I care about the state of the world and the people who dwell therein, and I am capable of proclaiming that care over and over again using the platform my privilege provides me.

After years of trial and error, I can even plan a fundraiser for the distant victims of a natural disaster, organize a public protest, or bring some helpful vim and vigor to worthy debates around board-room tables. I can probably even propose an excessively ego-attached game plan with ten simple steps to make whatever broken thing we are observing together a teensy bit more whole. Like many progres-sive utopian dreamers before me, I am capable of pontificating about a whole new world when the occasion arises.

Yet, every Sunday the people I serve come up to silently light candles for the deeply held struggles and the evolving triumphs of their lives. They do this without the slightest glimmer of perfor-mance or display. They do it with tears in their eyes and a wobble in their hands. They do it with confidence and fear and the world-weary glances that I know to be evidence of their grief. They do all of this not because they want to be a part of something perfect or vi-sionary or high-vaunted, but because the doing of it heals something in their souls that is and has always been precious.

And so they come up to the chancel in our temple of mid-century design, all full of the sheer horror and glory of being human, and I press their hands with unperformed and authentic devotion before I light a single candle of my own.

"For those who tend the vineyards," I say silently, while the flame catches and grows. For all those who labor in the fields of liberal idealism. For the ones who work the plows of this fertile soil. For the ones to whom blessings are not yet extended in this whole new world we are building together. For the ones who went before us, and the ones who are still waiting to be included in the dream, I light a little flame, and I am both grateful for and daunted by the work that lies ahead.

Two

Twentieth-Century Modernists in the Twenty-First-Century Church

> Because democracy exalts freedom, not dogma, it can be world-uniting. The attempt to unite the world upon the basis of dogma, whether political, religious, or any other kind, is sure to fail. Dogma divides. It is dogma that is dividing the world now. . . . Democracy, however, which converts the war-to-the-death of dogma into the peaceful conflict of opinion, can provide the world with unity.
>
> —A. Powell Davies[13]

Despite the aforementioned dis-ease that jangled around in my heart long after seminary was over, when I walked out of the academy and into parish ministry, neither the failure of the Owenite dream nor the decreasing relevance of the liberal church's utopian optimism appeared on my own radar screen. I was mostly just trying to figure out how the copy machine worked.

In those early days of ministry, the only thing that saved me from my utter ignorance was the fact that I was gathered up into community by a group of fellow young pastors, representing the denominational spectrum. We were all in our first parishes, all still trying to figure it out. Together, we were almost ready to face everything to come in the lives of liberal pastors, even though the nature of these challenges was completely unknown to us at the time.

As young pastors in liberal Protestant traditions, our own modest racial, ethnic, and socioeconomic diversity generally represented the modest racial, ethnic, and socioeconomic diversity in the churches we would be called to serve. We were mostly white, mostly middle class, mostly native English speakers, and mostly progressive. The more ideologically conservative or unbendingly radical among us tended to drop off as the work wore on, leaving us to gel as a deep and theologically rigorous lot, each of us committed Gen X denizens of whatever land it was that liberal religion marched toward.

In those days, we could still quote Habermas and Hegel on demand because the sheen of schoolwork still gleamed on our unwrinkled brows. We could debate the real presence in the Eucharist—or lack thereof—without feeling awkward in the least, because doctrinal differences that sent our ancestors into apoplexy became half-joking and deeply studied asides in the greater arc of our shared anxieties and hopes.

We were postmodern enough to be just a little bit bored with postmodernism, diligent enough to take the liturgies and theological commitments of our religious traditions seriously, and progressive enough to know that, on the most essential level, we were all engaged in the same project of shaping the future of liberal religion together.

Since we saw ourselves as something akin to post-postmodernists, we also tended to yearn together for a measure of liturgical tradition we felt many of our churches had attempted to leave behind. We wanted to reclaim the language and forms of worship that grounded us in the history of our unique traditions while never abandoning the theological and social progressivism that lay at the heart of our callings.

While our racial, ethnic, and socioeconomic diversity ran nearly parallel to the demographics of the congregations we served, we were a generation or two younger than most of the people in the pews. Unlike us, our parishioners still identified with the tail end of what had been a vibrant, challenging, and theologically rich modernist era in liberal Protestantism—a modernist era in which, frankly, we had never lived.

We were spiritually starving Gen Xers serving an aging population of Baby Boomer radicals, trying to bridge the gaps between who we were, who we served, and who we were collectively called to be.

Since the congregations we served tended to regularly lift up the memory and example of the true modernist era of progressive American Protestantism, there were ways in which those congregations telegraphed to us exactly who it was we were *supposed* to be and—more or less—what kind of word we were *supposed* to be about. Handily enough, who we were supposed to be as a worshipping body was pretty much exactly what they had been since just after the end of World War II—namely, good twentieth-century modernists. And what we were supposed to be about was a continued proclamation of the dream first articulated by the modernist preachers in the generations before our arrival on the scene.

In the early twentieth century, modernism in the liberal church was a bold departure from the orthodoxies of a post-enlightenment confessional age. It was characterized by the overlaying of rational philosophical thought atop traditional biblical exegesis, the alignment of reason and religion, and a willingness to hold dogmas of all sorts up to the greater test of human experience.

Liberal Christians in the modernist era followed the prophetic voices of theologians like Walter Rauschenbusch, who most clearly claimed that liberal theology was more than an experiment in visionary idealism, it was also a call to address the pressing social problems of its time. His 1907 work *Christianity and the Social Crisis* made the case that progressive Christians were called to step up and claim nothing less radical than a controlling stake in the social forces of American life—all aimed at bringing about a more harmonious and less exploitative way of being in the world.

In 1922, the young firebrand preacher Harry Emerson Fosdick stood before his congregation at First Presbyterian Church of New York and formally demarcated the battle lines between the modernist liberals and the opposing forces, which had only recently come to be known as the "fundamentalists."

His sermon *Shall the Fundamentalists Win?* was printed and reprinted all around the country. Somehow in that single address he managed to knock almost every sacred cow in the fundamentalist canon from its pedestal. On his list of unnecessary pre-modern idols were the virgin birth, the millennial expectation of Christ's return, and the assumed inerrancy of the Christian scriptures. He took it all on, while offering clear a critique of the general ethos of pessimism and impending sin-driven doom espoused within fundamentalist circles.

By 1925, knowing that Fosdick was unlikely to compromise his progressive theology to make nice with the Presbyterian mainstream, John D. Rockefeller built the man his own church, where he filled the pulpit for another sixteen years. This was Riverside Church in New York City, still one of the flagships of progressive Protestantism today.

It was at Riverside in 1935 that Fosdick once again upended expectations by preaching another barn burner of a sermon that dismantled certain idols lifted up in place of authentic good news.

This barn burner, however, wasn't aimed at the fundamentalist opponents he faced in the great sparring match of his earlier work. Instead, in a text titled *The Church Must Go Beyond Modernism*, he took to task the tendency among religious liberals to use the tools of the progressive tradition as a means of letting themselves off the hook.

He said we had misused the liberal gospel by allowing ourselves to look away from our own utter dependence upon God and our deep complicity in systems of oppression. From there on out, Fosdick demanded that those who had extended his own fierce modernism into a mishmash of sunny optimism rethink their approach. By the end of his preaching life, he dedicated himself to reimagining both individual and collective sin within the wider framework of liberal theology.

That was in 1935—when modernist optimism had already reached its apex and socially engaged, neo-orthodox theologians like Reinhold Niebuhr had become conversation partners to the progressive mainstream. By that time, even Fosdick, perhaps the most eloquent framer of American religious modernism, had concluded something was amiss in the ever-hopeful heart of liberal progress.

Fosdick died knowing that the next step for all religious liberals was not to return to an orthodox conception of scripture, revelation, or atonement. Instead, he believed we must reclaim our ability to stand in the presence of collective tragedy, systematic oppression, and personal sinfulness without sunnily reframing it into a narrative of illimitable progress. He proclaimed that this could only happen through the application of humility and grace, and that this would bring with it both deep discomfort and abundant change.

Again, that was in 1935.

My Gen X colleagues of various denominational identities gathered together for the first time in 2004, so some significant time had passed. Yet, many of the congregations we served on the left of the Protestant religious spectrum—including an outright majority of those in my own Unitarian Universalist tradition—still spoke of themselves as a modern, progressive tonic for the pre-modern unscientific orthodoxies that continued to preach their bloody atonements and tests of faith.

Even after the turn of the twenty-first century, we were still pretty much expected to show up on Sunday mornings and preach reimagined versions of Fosdick's greatest hits from the 1920s. Our Sunday schools, while grounded in specific and distinct theologies, often served primarily as places to inoculate children against the fundamentalism that their parents felt besieged by in the broader culture. Our worship, while traditional in most liturgical senses, was best received when it was bright with a theological vision of human progress, social commitment, and scientific advancement.

We sprinkled our fundamentally modernist takedowns of pre-modern orthodoxy with some references to Oprah's Book Club and the latest Star Trek movie. But underneath it all, we still expended a fair amount of effort on recasting fundamentalist desolation into liberal hopefulness. We cooled the heat of dour brimstone so that some bright but nonburning sunshine might peek through.

As my colleague Tom Schade put it recently in an issue of the Unitarian Universalist denominational magazine,

> In the middle of the twentieth century, when contemporary Unitarian Universalism was formed, our public theology was shaped by our resistance to the public civic Christianity of the day. . . . We believed in "deeds not creeds" and in building heaven on Earth and in "social action." We were militants about the separation of church and state. We were increasingly drawn toward an oppositional stance in society. On a theological level, we were quite content to be sure of what we didn't believe and much more vague about what we did believe.[14]

A modernist vision. A progressive tonic for a conservative world. A hair shirt to itch the holy hell out of the complacent and the pious and the phony. In 2004, we were all of those things, even when the high water mark of the modernist era was fifty years behind us.

Some of our most vibrant congregations in those days were more than a little raucous, often cranky, and full of the agitational energy of self-identified outsiders. Like the Owenite social reformers in my hometown and the Boston Brahmins in their well-appointed salons before us, we dwelled within an ideological landscape that allowed us to imagine ourselves as rebellious visionaries of a whole new world. All while we were planted squarely within the mainstream of this world's privilege and power.

Now let me acknowledge—because my snarkiness can carry me away—progressive Protestantism has been taking the modernist stand against pre-enlightenment fundamentalism for about a hundred years, and it is an altogether worthy enterprise. The contribution made by the twentieth-century modernists to the broader scope of American religion is significant enough to humble a mere dabbler such as myself, and some of the reforms they set out to create within the American churches are by no means complete.

Fundamentalism in all its forms is not dead. While I might argue that the modernists have essentially won that particular debate, the soul-shrinking orthodoxies that Fosdick and his allies knocked off their pedestals almost a hundred years ago have indeed risen in insidious ways in our own time.

This exact forward-looking modernism of human uplift was among the things I loved most about my Unitarian Universalist tradition when it scooped me up and gave me a home twenty years ago.

It was still basically working then. Our churches were still on a general trend of upward growth. The good news that modernism existed to counter the fundamentalists was still a prophetic word that some people hadn't heard before. Some shadowed corners of superstition within our broader religious culture were still waiting for the light of reason to shine on through. Those shadowy corners exist even now, and the modernist/fundamentalist sparring match that has been afoot for the past hundred years is not altogether over.

The problem, however, is that this sparring match is no longer an adequate reason for liberal religion to go on existing. If, even after the turn of the twenty-first century, we were still striving to be the very best early twentieth-century modernist progressives we could be, clearly there were voices we were not yet fully listening to.

Cultivated, Educated White Men

As the liberal church re-formed itself alongside the needs and visions of aging baby boomers, its late twentieth-century congregations were full of self-professed boundary pushers who were comfortably, if querulously, ensconced in institutions that proclaimed boldness while remaining fundamentally conservative.

Like the artists and hippies and artisanal soap makers walking their labyrinths in modern-day New Harmony, we were holding down the fort of progressive liberalism against the incursions of old-school fire and brimstone. And we were so grateful to have found such a lovely, eccentric, even quaint place to hang out together.

I too found a home there among the safely rebellious authority-eschewing anti-institutionalists. Even at the turn of the twenty-first century, I was welcomed into fellowship and leadership within the confines of the not-so-radical mid-century modernist church. It gave me a pulpit and meaningful work to do, and I was honored to take my place in a long line of those who marched out of the mists of superstition and into the bright new day that was always just about to dawn right here, among us.

There were days, during that era, when we stood out on the street corners with our signs against the invasion of Iraq, and it felt like the drums of war might really stop beating. Even when they didn't, we took pride in the fact that we were at the center of the opposition, speaking out hope for a different kind of nation, where xenophobia didn't have to be a reflexive response to fear and terror didn't have to turn us into tyrants. We were still there, living out a vision of a different kind of church where nobody had to earn their way to blessedness and the burnishing glow of community was available to all who would come to the table we ourselves had set.

There were times, in those days, where we could almost grasp what that other, less fearful, nation might be like. There were times when we could almost feel the pure possibility of a different way.

There were times, with some mild delusions of grandeur, when I could almost see myself walking in the footsteps of the glorious modernist preachers before me—people like A. Powell Davies, who believed that, "democracy, exalt[ing] freedom" could unite the world and glorious human imagination could be traded for nightmare.[15]

I believed in the upward vision of history sometimes—especially when we sang songs of those who went before, moving rank by rank to advance greater knowledge. I took part in a faithful witness to the ever-expanding dream of freedom when we marched and marched and marched again for marriage equality, justice for migrant laborers, living wages, housing equity, and all the rest.

But of course, the old cynicisms of my seminary days couldn't stay buried forever. Sometimes my uneasiness was just that—cynicism, of the stripe that led me to work year after year for marriage equality while never fully believing that a federal amendment establishing gay marriage could or would pass in the foreseeable future.

Even after working on it for years, I was still surprised when our efforts yielded the full federal protection we had professed as our ultimate goal. Sometimes my cynicism was just cynicism.

And sometimes it was not. Sometimes it was the creeping reality that this unending progress we had so long espoused was just another kind of story, a tale we told the children so they did not have to be afraid.

I never bought into the Whiggish narrative of history's inevitable progress that had evolved from modernist roots into a brightly lit justice-centered teleology for the liberal church, but I wanted to. I loved it even if I couldn't believe it. And I served it, even when I knew the abstract project of unending human progress through the advancement of privileged liberal ideals was just as flawed, just as biased, and just as doomed as the utopias from which I arose.

The Owenites on the Boatload of Knowledge had espoused similar reformist ideals long before the birth of the Protestant Social Gospel. They invested their time, money, and significant capacity into the effort to build a perfect society because they truly believed, deep down in their secular souls, that such a perfect society was possible. They held to this faith because they too were standing in midst of a lineage that long preceded them.

In the era leading up to the rising of utopian sentiment that birthed the New Harmony experiment, the French and industrial revolutions worked together to create a powerful post-enlightenment faith in science, reason, and human capacity on both sides of the Atlantic.

This meant that the decades before the American Civil War gave rise to a whole generation of thinkers who were prepared to take the newly harnessed power of the scientific method and make use of it in wider fields like sociology, city planning, education, government, and law.

This progressive vision for society and its institutions became a new kind of religion that was bigger than, and warily inclusive of, the liberal church. Historian Pankaj Mishra has called this nineteenth-century secular faith a newborn cult of "development" that necessarily prized scientific and intellectual advancement while simultaneously deconstructing the old accretions of power that centered traditional religious practice.[16]

And so was born a hybrid tradition within the liberal church. Melding secular scientific progressivism with liberal theological interpretations of received tradition, the whole thing was united by a nearly unshakable faith in the upward-moving development of history. This tradition claimed that new light would supplant old superstitions and new efforts would guide the people closer to the always-approaching heaven-on-earth that could and would be created by *cultivated, educated, white men* with the means, the breeding, and the vision to bring their ideals to their ultimate and glorious fruition.

Why *cultivated . . . educated . . . white . . . men?* Because almost all the most widely celebrated scions of both enlightenment rationalism and twentieth-century modernism our progressive tradition set us up to revere were exactly that—cultivated, educated, white men. Their framing of issues was predicated on the work of similarly cultivated, educated, white men who came before them. Thus, their perceptions were limited in very similar ways to those of the educated elites on the Boatload of Knowledge.

In their book *Saving Paradise*, theologians Rebecca Ann Parker and Rita Nakashima Brock contemplate the ways in which the development of the progressive churches was compromised by the limited perceptions of their great white male thinkers. They point out that in the Unitarian tradition, William Ellery Channing, the greatest among our nineteenth-century preachers and theologians, was quick to articulate a high opinion of human nature as made in the image of the divine, but altogether slow to admit that such divinity existed in those held in chattel slavery.

Eventually goaded by those who were influenced by this theology, including prominent women in his church, Channing did ultimately join the rallying cry of abolitionism. Yet even then, after forty years spent defining American Protestant progressivism from his pulpit, that stand cost him his position as minister to the economically privileged, white, merchant-class people who filled his congregation's membership rolls.[17]

The stone walls of Channing's church were held up by the money of those who benefited financially from chattel slavery for generations. Harry Emerson Fosdick's temple of modernism at Riverside Church was financed by the oil money of a robber baron. Washington DC's New York Avenue Presbyterian Church, while proclaiming a boldly modernist vision, also became the de rigueur gathering place for the District's gilded-age elite.

In American religious life, it had ever been so. This alignment of progressive religious idealism with the very forces of conservative economic status quo that their socially progressive vision and increasingly liberal theology would ostensibly decry was nothing new. Optimistic assumptions around society's progress have been tied up with the maintaining of middle-class comforts for quite some time.

Writing in 1976 of the way in which modernists in the liberal churches reconciled the seeming struggle between science and religion, James Luther Adams noted that,

> Progress and evolution were acceptable ideas since they gave an explanation of the achievement of mankind as the result of a long and arduous struggle, and they opened endless vistas into the future—"the progress of mankind onward and upward forever." The foundation of scientific humanism is obviously here, as are the bases for a middle-class philosophy of history and the defense of private property as individuals transcend themselves to gain control over all that is around them.[18]

In the pre-WWI era, the foundation of our emerging utopian vision was already there. The foundation for all of it—for the humanistic uplift that gives us hope for a bright future, for the bold human progress in which we can forthrightly believe, and for the safely hidebound middle-class conservatism that twists itself so easily into domination and dominion.

When viewed purely through the lens of abstract and universalizing measurements, that utopian vision was altogether founded, perhaps even earthshakingly successful. Steven Pinker, a contemporary public intellectual, has used data analysis to show that people live longer, eat better, take more vacations, and enjoy much better dental health than denizens of a pre-enlightenment age. With these indisputable measurements, he argues that the twentieth-century project of benevolent uplift has basically worked. There are a great many generalized data sets to prove it. From ten thousand feet above the ground, the facts don't lie. It only gets tricky when we move down from the vantage point of general trends and toward the specific circumstances of people's lives.

Building toward his much-vaunted recent work, *Enlightenment Now*, Pinker has gone so far as to declare the Tuskegee Syphilis Experiment as an isolated case, rationalizing that the fatal racism that produced that experiment is subsumed by the larger optimistic trends his data show. In that infamous 1930s public health project, impoverished African-American men were studied through the untreated progression of the disease without any informed consent.

Pinker seems to understand that act as collateral damage on the way toward improved health outcomes for the broadest spectrum of the American public. Who are we to compare the "one-time failure to prevent harm to a few dozen people with the prevention of hundreds of millions of deaths per century, in perpetuity."[19]

In this way, Pinker seems to imply that some people just have to take the hit, since the cost of each individual injustice pales in comparison to the larger project. What neither he nor most of the progressive luminaries of twentieth-century religious modernism are willing to admit when they proclaim inevitable progress is that the same people always seem to take that hit. And the same people always seem to garner the greatest rewards.

Pinker's failure comes in his persistent refusal to acknowledge that we can and must do better. Human lives don't pale in comparison to the grand abstraction of enlightenment progress. When we say that immigrants, children, women, and people of color cannot be collateral damage in the swinging arc of history, it is not a detail or a nit that needs picking. It is the necessary corrective that keeps enlightenment optimism from running away with itself down the well-trodden path of exploitation and privilege.

One cannot deny the benefits of enlightenment rationalism nor the quality-of-life improvements wrought by a scientific age. The progressive church of the modern era has been utterly transformed by those enlightenment ideals—but the church is also called to higher things. As such, we don't have the luxury of lazily denying that even our most successful progressive reforms have systematically excluded—and sometimes even preyed upon—the people who do not already stand at the center of power.

And there you have it. An oft-unacknowledged arc of history that doesn't seem quite so triumphant; a narrative of the liberal church that stands counter to the rampart-holding optimism we proclaim in our most stirring hymns.

If we put our thought-train into reverse and play the scenario out from the current moment backward over the course of several generations of American religious thinkers, the sequence of events is clear.

Well past the beginning of the twenty-first century, liberal churches continued to remember the good old days of twentieth-century modernism. The great modernist churches of the mid-twentieth century were tied to the concept of unending societal potential birthed after the industrial revolution. That vision of unending societal potential was in turn tied to patriarchal and racially unjust systems that benefited from the oppression they decried.

The prevailing cultural and socioeconomic ethos of this gospel of unending progress was built by and for white men with significant power. They exercised that power through seemingly benevolent dominion over the earth, its peoples, and its mysteries alike.

So, that explains a lot of things.

A Wider Welcome

Like the dead utopia of my hometown, the twentieth-century modernist utopian vision was doomed by its persistent refusal to place itself and its reforms within a broader social location. As philosopher

Stephen Toulmin describes it, modernity tends to frame questions in "terms that are independent of context."[20]

That lack of context meant that the modernists among us never did manage to own up to their own privileged social location, nor to fully acknowledge the domination of the natural world assumed in a theology that preaches unending human progress. Somewhere near the end of the twentieth century, when we were all busy celebrating our anti-authoritarianism and performing safely benign forms of social radicalism, we—the anointed and culturally conservative inheritors of the modernist Protestant tradition—were outpaced in both theological rigor and spiritual authenticity by experiential and intersectional movements among and between people of color across and beyond the religious spectrum.

The problem eating at the heart of the modernist religious utopia has always been this—the table progressive religion invites everyone to, no matter how broad and expansive it may be, is almost always set by people who believe they are white. Those same white people who set the table have chosen to repeatedly align that white identity with the predominant power structures of their day.

Among the difficult truths we are called to grapple with is the fact that oppressive power structures undergird every single era of progressive optimism in this country. Spanning from the utopians who first landed in New Harmony to the pulpits young preachers occupy today, the great institutions of liberal faith were and are inextricably interconnected with systems of supremacy, patriarchy, and oppression. Acknowledging this reality does not have to undo us. But remaining insensate and unrepentant in the face of it just might do exactly that.

Within my own Unitarian Universalist tradition, our prevailing white, middle-class culture has long related to the voices of people of color, queer theorists, liberationists, and feminist/womanist theologians as inputs from the outside. We attend to them when it is easy, lift them up when their witness fits within *our* larger project of reform, and are convicted by them only when *they* take the time and expend the energy to stare into the tired eyes of mostly white institutions and keep staring until those institutions are the first to blink.

The time has come to take this liberal theology of ours, a sacred inheritance from all who came before, and submit it to the transformation that comes along with a consequential commitment. The time has come to shift away from benevolent paternalism of the sort that fundraises *for* and organizes rallies *for* the people at the margins and toward a willingness to listen and respond *to* the voices that have historically been cast out of the center of our utopian vision.

If this progressive dream of ours is not to die, if brown, black, queer, trans, migrant female bodies are not to be sacrificed on the altar of democracy while religious progressives hang out together and celebrate our counter-culturalism, the center needs to shift.

Three

The Myth of Inevitable Progress

I find these days that a wistful form of time travel has become a persistent political theme, both on the right and on the left. On November 10 *The New York Times* reported that nearly seven in ten Republicans prefer America as it was in the 1950s, a nostalgia of course entirely unavailable to a person like me, for in that period I could not vote, marry my husband, have my children, work in the university I work in, or live in my neighborhood. Time travel is a discretionary art: a pleasure trip for some and a horror story for others. Meanwhile some on the left have time travel fancies of their own, imagining that the same rigid ideological principles once applied to the matters of workers' rights, welfare, and trade can be applied unchanged to a globalized world of fluid capital.

—Zadie Smith[21]

I once heard a beloved female preacher muse about the fact that each generation of clergy are blessed and burdened with the task of interpreting the events of their own age. As preachers and pastors, our daily work involves interpreting those events through the theological and moral frameworks we are given. We are also given the daunting task of expanding or altering those frameworks in light of the world-changing and heartbreaking events of our own time.

This colleague spoke with a catch in her throat about what it meant for her generation of pastors to serve during the AIDS epidemic: worrying together as the symptoms first appeared, fighting together for the rights of the suffering, and weeping together as they repeatedly gathered to bury the ones they had loved and lost. There are defining moments for each generation of pastors and preachers, events that only that generation can interpret firsthand.

Before her generation, the prominent pastors who bore the blessing and the burden of interpreting America's stories from behind America's pulpits were mostly men. They had the unenviable task of preaching their way through Vietnam, Japanese-American internment camps, the Kent State shootings, and the Cuban Missile Crisis. They were left to interpret and expound upon the Civil Rights Movement, the Jim Crow era, and the strange fruit hanging on Southern trees. Before them, the great modernists sought to find meaning in the blood-drenched horrors of Eastern Europe, the explosion of the atom bomb, and the rebuilding of nations from the rubble of a world at war.

The events each generation is given to interpret are not placed against one another like a contest in the immensity of tragic circumstances. Over time, the work of interpreting tragedy and adapting tradition has not fundamentally shifted, and my generation is obviously neither the first nor the last to stand before the world's events and find that our received traditions feel hollow in the face of such suffering. Gen Xers like me are not the most blessed nor the most burdened of generational cohorts.

And yet, even knowing that we are hardly unique, let's just say it like it is: the events of our own age feel nothing short of . . . well, biblical. As I write this, Mexico is digging out from two of the deadliest earthquakes in a hundred years, the Western United States is burning with uncontained fires, and two hurricanes bear down with unyielding force on the Gulf Coast. All of this while deportations loom for immigrant dreamers who have spent their lives as taxpaying Americans, children are being torn away from their parents at the borders of our country, xenophobia and rampant nationalism have spread like a virus throughout the democratic world, and the looming specter of nuclear armament continues to hang over our heads.

Meanwhile, the nonindictment of another police officer in the taking of yet another young Black life swirls beneath the currents of our everyday lives, and the banners declaring "Black Lives Matter" hang on the grassy lawns outside of our churches even as we struggle to comprehend and overcome the insidious white supremacy that is still within them.

We are poised here amid history, grappling with the legacy of faithful optimism and belief in American progress that our predecessors left for us, blessed and burdened with finding meaning during these times.

Given the state of this world as we know it, it is difficult to honestly preach the fundamentally utopian idealism of the charismatic white men who came before us. We don't want to preach the old progressive narrative of continual advance because we do not want to lie.

In the life of the churches I have served, I've always suspected that if there is one thing the people in the pews can perceive and respond to, even on a subconscious and visceral level, it is a leader who isn't telling them the truth.

Relatedly, those who come to our churches searching for meaning can recognize an honest word when they hear it. It may not be the honest word they want to hear—it may not even be an honest word that I particularly want to preach—but somewhere behind even my own hesitancy and their occasional discomfort, the honesty itself must shine through.

This honest word, spoken from behind a pulpit built for truth telling, cannot long survive the lingering miasma of bullshit, and, while it may well offer comfort in both personal and collective crisis, it cannot promote the safety of denial. I fail to proclaim something truly honest every Sunday. I'm not sure I ever could, but the intention to do so remains an impossibly holy struggle that every leader in the liberal church should submit to.

This is the work of leadership in these times, to interpret the events of the era in a way that is both honest and soul sustaining. It is a challenge that does not belong solely to preachers but to teachers, non-profit managers, store clerks, and presidents. We are the meaning-makers for one another, and we should not be surprised when the struggle to make meaning demands of us honest leadership over and over again.

But We've Come So Far, Haven't We?

Shortly after the results of the 2016 election, then-President Barack Obama gathered his staff members and asked them to attend an impromptu summit in the Oval Office. The whole place was understandably in an uproar. Young staffers stood in the hallways staring blankly into space. Sideways glances met tear-shrouded eyes. Everyone wanted to know what had happened, and when they came together to hear the message the boss himself had to share, it was a vision of history that stood in poetic counterpoint to the whispered fearful conversations they may have heard that week in their liberal congregations and progressive coffee shops.

"This is not the apocalypse," Obama told them.

Writing about it later in the *New Yorker*, David Remnick pieced together staffer recollections of that moment. According to him, Obama said that "history does not move in straight lines; sometimes it goes sideways, sometimes it goes backward."[22] When he later queried Obama about the dose of comfort he doled out on that day, the president responded, "I don't believe in apocalyptic—until the apocalypse comes. I think nothing is the end of the world until the end of the world."

Indeed, along with the progressives and liberals who came before him, Obama was not ready to throw in the towel on his vision of a progressive future. There was, he insisted, no point in endlessly looking back to dissect what led up the moment when the will of the average white American voter was ultimately revealed. It was what it was. It had always been so. It was not the apocalypse. But neither, on some fundamental level, was it all that much of a surprise. History had gone sideways this time around, and for many who had seen it go sideways before, it was not a new experience.

At this time in our nation's history, white, right-leaning conservative voters tend to think things have gone not sideways in the past few decades, but quite a bit downhill. Things were better way back when. When it was simpler, I suppose. When it was easier to see who was in charge.

English author Zadie Smith reported that just before the votes were cast in the 2016 presidential election, nearly 70 percent of Republicans stated that they would "prefer America as it was in the 1950s."[23] Seen through this lens, one form of popular white people time travel is regressive, reaching back before the Civil Rights era to shirtwaist dresses, curlers in ladies' hair, and the genteel racism that provided a polite front for ongoing lynching.

To progressives in the modernist era and beyond, the penchant for time travel is no less apparent. The key difference is that progressive time travel fantasies tend to go in the opposite direction. As progressives have learned ever since the Enlightenment, history goes forward. History is on the march. Progress, especially American progress, is all but inevitable if we just hang on for the ride. According to our received framework of historical progress, not only is this moment in our history not the apocalypse, it is barely a blip on the upward trajectory of the human endeavor. After all—we've come so far, haven't we?

This forward-looking progressive time travel can also bring along with it a lazily exhausted idealism that emerges when people of privilege wonder out loud if we can't move on from talking about these oppressions already and focus on something more pleasant. After all, this is indeed not the end of the world. And did I mention we have come so far?

From this point in time back into the receding mists, history goes in one direction or another and reaches out to convict the present either of too much innovation or not enough vision. People of privilege can engage in either form of time travel. It is possible that they have always been capable of this magic.

Ecologist Paul Kingsnorth writes, "The elites of ancient Rome or the Indus Valley civilization or Ur of the Chaldeans doubtless believed that the arc of justice was bending towards their own world-view, too, but it didn't, in the end."[24]

Kingsnorth has joined with other thinkers and writers who are convinced that we have already reached the tipping point of environmental degradation that previous generations of ecologists once warned us of. In fact, he sees himself as a sort of post-ecologist—inhabiting whatever creative space comes next when traditional notions of ecological preservation have failed. He and other thinkers alongside him are quite certain that the clock of environmental degradation cannot be either turned back or paused. Nor can we look outward toward some better future by adhering to the liberal notions of progress that undergird the whole of the Western tradition. To him, these notions of limitless progress are pretty much what got us into this mess to begin with:

> The myth of progress is to us what the myth of god-given warrior prowess was to the Romans, or the myth of eternal salvation was to the conquistadors: without it, our efforts cannot be sustained. Onto the root stock of Western Christianity, the Enlightenment at its most optimistic grafted a vision of an Earthly paradise, towards which human effort guided by calculative reason could take us. Following this guidance, each generation will live a better life than the life of those that went before it. History becomes an escalator, and the only way is up. On the top floor is human perfection. It is important that this should remain just out of reach in order to sustain the sensation of motion.[25]

And so, the inheritors of conservative fundamentalist ideologies retain their equilibrium by looking back into a period of history when people like them held power more overtly. Meanwhile, the privileged inheritors of the Enlightenment tradition maintain their sensation of motion and purpose by looking ahead, toward a perfect future they can build with their own hands.

Since this is indeed not the apocalypse, since nothing is the end until the end, we tell ourselves the same old story of inevitable progress. We believe that the escalator is still ascending, even as we ourselves stand motionless and rather bewildered upon it.

The Stories We Tell

We tell ourselves the story of inevitable progress in part because we know that stories are powerful, world-shaping things. Our stories about history and human nature shape not only who we think we are, but who we actually are in relation to the people and the ecosystems around us. Since we are the ones who tell the stories, we often imagine that we are also the ones who control them, but the interesting and sometimes terrifying truth is that it is most often precisely the other way around.

The stories we tell, and the symbols and language we use to tell them, give rise to the way we understand ourselves. In some sense, we human beings cannot even know who we are in a vacuum separated from the stories we tell about the world and our place in it.

In what modern philosophy has sometimes called "the linguistic turn," we are made and remade by the words we use and the meanings we ascribe to them. Likewise, biology shows that the neural pathways of our brains are not independent structures that exist outside of the language and symbols that course through them. The way we think is directly shaped by the stories we tell. In this way, our stories create our worldviews. They tell us who we are and reinforce themselves over generations.

And so, the story of upward and onward progress that is so prominent in today's progressive churches, one passed down to us from the European Enlightenment tradition, has created privileged religious liberalism in its own image. We become who we say we are. We expect this story to be true and we pass it on. Yet, with the continued passage of this progressive story from one generation to another comes a set of expectations and entitlements that in turn shape the way we live as people of faith in this beautiful and woebegone world.

This story of continual and uninterrupted progress inculcates an expectation that each successive generation of working-class Americans should see a way of life that is fundamentally easier for them than it was for the generation who immediately preceded them. It generates a collective entitlement to the good life that entrenches itself in the middle-class heart and comes out fighting when its hopes, dreams, ambitions, and dictates are not realized.

Writer and social commentator Ta-Nehisi Coates has said that the dominant groups in American society tend to absorb the ongoing economic tribulations of people of color without widespread or evident objection. But he notes that the same cannot be said when economic circumstances result in a generational lack of opportunity for the white laboring class. Somehow the divine and cosmic order maintains its shape when people of color cannot achieve generational advancement, but "when white workers suffer, something in nature has gone awry."[26]

This fierce resistance encountered when the escalator of opportunity stops going ever-upward for white working-class people implies an ongoing faith, present within nearly all economic strata of white-identified American culture, in the story we have been telling ourselves since at least the end of World War II.

That story, of course, is one of democratic advancement and unceasing economic opportunity for people who have already experienced generations of the same. When expectations of such continued advancement are simultaneously met with changing economic realities and authentic demand from people at the margins to make space for simple equanimity, those with systemic privilege see it as an oppression or curtailment of their freedom. White people can come to perceive this change in shifting resources as a form of personal attack. The story we tell has shaped us, and we do not know who we are if the truth of that story is no longer evident. In fact, we may feel that our very identity is under siege.

As noted antiracist lecturer and educator Tim Wise says, "When you've had the luxury of presuming yourself to be the norm, the prototype of an American, any change in the demographic and cultural realities in your society will strike you as outsized attacks on your status. . . . When you're used to 90 percent or more of the pie, having to settle for only 75 or 70 percent? Oh my God, it's like the end of the world."[27]

Pushed steadily from behind by systematic privilege at the highest level throughout American history, the escalator of progress for the people who are conditioned to the identity of whiteness goes up and up—until it doesn't. When finally it doesn't, white Americans go casting about for someone to blame, never quite realizing their own received mythologies of time and history have something to do with both their economic struggles and the depth of their own racially tinged anger.

After the 2016 presidential election, progressives and moderate conservatives alike quickly pointed toward the Democratic party's supposed abandonment of the white working voter as the cause of America's unsettling swing toward nativism and xenophobia. In this way, the suffering of the nation was blamed on coastal elites and ivory-tower academics who were so out of touch with the heartland of America that they didn't even notice white people's suffering. Meanwhile, the Republican candidate fueled the virtually undimmed white supremacy of the nation by proclaiming the inherent death-dealing danger of any immigrant with more melanin than a latter-day Nordic Viking. These cycles of blame shifting and xenophobia gain power and authority from the long-standing myth of inevitable white progress at the heart of American democracy.

The promise of inevitable progress in American history, or Western history in general, is a false narrative that people of color both inside and outside of the church have long risen to challenge. Liberation theologians in the Catholic and Protestant traditions have spent decades challenging the perception that neo-liberal economics naturally lead to progress in either Latin American communities or Central American democracies. The literature is voluminous and widely available.

But privileged people go to great lengths to protect their own self-shaping stories, and often the progressive left has a hard time receiving the simple truth-telling of leaders of color.

Within my own Unitarian Universalist tradition, Mark Morrison-Reed is the primary documentarian of those many African-American voices that have so often gone unheeded within the denomination's narrative histories. He's collected and published their stories to remind us that non-white voices, stories from the margins, and powerful Black-centered narratives actually do exist within liberal religious history and identity.

On the fiftieth anniversary of the march on Selma, at which many progressive Protestants heeded the call to march with Martin Luther King, Morrison-Reed spoke to a gathered company of faithful progressives who were preparing to board buses to Selma and walk in the actual footsteps of the civil rights leaders who went before them.

Speaking from the depth of his scholarly research and from his experience as an African-American minister in a white-dominated tradition, he lifted up the significant ways that Unitarian involvement in Selma truly changed the people who were there. He said that what it changed, most of all, was our progressive movement's expectation of ourselves.

To many Black leaders in the faith, the Unitarian Universalist presence in Selma telegraphed that the denomination was finally ready to meet history and its persistent struggle without shrinking away into white, middle-class comforts. It was a signal that perhaps their always-hopeful tradition was finally willing to stay in the troubled waters in abiding relationship to those who were drowning. Black leaders thought that it was an opportunity to take the next step in the evolution of their own vision for the faith tradition they loved.

Because of this, Morrison-Reed said that the aftermath of Selma and the height of the civil rights movement marked an important turning point in the approach of African-American leaders within the Unitarian Universalist tradition. It was the moment, he said, when Black leadership shifted from "integration to self-determination." Finally, Black leaders thought, they could stop going along to get along with the white majority in their progressive congregations and guide the course of the future on terms they could actually set for themselves.

In less than four years, that shift toward self-determination proved to be something our optimistic and forward-reaching denomination was not fully prepared to accept. In 1968, after initially supporting denominational funding for Black-organized efforts within Unitarian Universalism to fight their own political repression and champion their own cultural expression, associational leadership encountered sharp internal criticism in a variety of forms.

In 1969, singed by the claim that Black caucusing was tantamount to both "separatism" and some form of reverse discrimination, the primarily white leadership of the denomination voted to sharply curtail that funding for Black caucus groups, shifting away from self-determination and back into the conservative hope for integration into the larger, white-dominated culture of the liberal church.

The old story of upward historical progress laid over a narrative of liberal white respectability reasserted itself all over again. The Unitarian Universalist Association wasn't ready for Black self-determination if Black self-determination meant it had to actually grapple with the legacy of its own racial history.

If it meant we had to take our eyes off the ever-rising escalator of rationalistic human advancement and look back at our own profound historical and contemporary limitations, it was a demand too burdensome for the comfortable white majority to accept.

In time, fighting for the self-determination they had risen to claim during the civil rights movement became the project of an unquiet and often unheeded body of Black leaders within the liberal church. Many grew exhausted by this fight. Many left, looking for environments outside of the liberal church, where their stories would be heard and their message would be welcomed with something other than moral caution and the continued preservation of white comfort.

Of course, Black public intellectuals had been busy disentangling an ideology of American advancement from its persistent false testimony to white innocence since long before the civil rights movement. Back at the turn of the twentieth century, even as he maintained something much like a modernist faithfulness in the advance of cultivated civilization, W.E.B. Dubois revealed the ways in which progress itself is built upon Black bodies.

Indeed, from the first ships that departed West Africa's shadowed gates of no return, to the tide of whiplashed labor that fueled the industrial revolution, and the continually running stream of money that upholds today's prison-industrial complex, the destruction of Black bodies is interwoven into America's national reality. To continue believing in the advancement of a fundamentally benevolent Western democracy would require a willingness to locate Black bodies outside of the very flow of history itself. DuBois poetically declared,

> We have seen,—Merciful God! in these wild days and in the name of Civilization, Justice and Motherhood—what have we not seen, right here in America, of orgy, cruelty, barbarism, and murder done to men and women of Negro descent.[28]

A progressive forward-leaning history of unremitting generational progress is, by its very nature, a white people's history, a story told by the dominant parties who wished, by means of propaganda and willful ignorance, to perpetuate their dominance into the next generation.

If privileged fundamentalists look back and privileged progressives look forward, the sins of our forebears and the achievements of our future selves are always beckoning on either side of the present moment. Regardless of our ideology, we can find someone to blame on either side of history—preferably someone who, conveniently enough, *is not us.*

But those at the margins of societal power cannot afford the luxury of ideological time travel. Those whose lives are on the line are trying to survive from one policy change to the next. They are literally trying to make it through the tumult of the next storm. They are trying to live where they are, not place their hope on a distant past or broadcast it out into a purely theoretical future.

For those nearer to the outside of empire than to the center of power, history moves neither forward nor back, but carries on in great violent lurches. It is experienced in uprisings and crackdowns, in waves of change and periods of complacency, in whole decades of playing by the rules and the unexpected moment when one must fight to survive. Time travel is not a luxury afforded to the oppressed, and an ideology that points to some other age is not salvific when this age we are presented with is all but unsurvivable.

Esperanza: To Hope without Triumph

Perhaps no one captures the oppressive nature of this upward-leaning, fundamentally hopeful "salvation history" better than social ethicist and progressive Baptist minister Miguel De La Torre, who advocates for a kind of awakened hopelessness.

De La Torre begins his definitive takedown of the progressivist view of history by reminding us that the English meaning of *hope* implies a kind of pausing in anticipation of something good that is about to be revealed. It is the breath before the upward motion, the stop on the way to inevitable wholeness. The Spanish translation of that word, however, gives a different meaning. *To hope* is translated as *esperar*, a word that asks us "to wait in apprehension of either good or evil."[29]

The distinction is important, given the differing experiences of progress and history often encountered by the oppressor and the oppressed. As De La Torre puts it,

> History is not defined through triumphant metanarratives, but instead is a kaleidoscope comprised of contradictory and complex untold stories and struggles of the very least among us who remain unnamed. History is full of stories of evil vanquishing good, brutality crushing peace. We presently live in a world that is not getting better for the global marginalized, rather, due to the widening wealth gap, [it is] getting worse."[30]

And yet, even when many in the global majority experience this widening wealth gap as a chasm that threatens to swallow them whole, the maintenance of future-oriented hopefulness in the middle-class project of continued growth remains a key priority in the liberal church. We tell the story of continued progress despite the experiences of people around us, and in so doing shape ourselves into a triumphal Easter faith that lets us live in the good news rather than fully joining together in an ongoing and unremitting struggle for justice.

As a preacher speaking into the activist reform tradition of his own Baptist faith, De La Torre reminds us that "The oppressed of the world occupy the space of Holy Saturday, the day after Friday's crucifixion, and the not yet Easter Sunday of resurrection."[31]

Guatemalan children struggling to survive in the midst of decimating gang violence cannot skip ahead during holy week. Migrant families stuck in a broken system cannot always hope in a way that naturally assumes a positive outcome. Unlike people of privilege in the liberal church, at the end of the day they cannot expect either an affirming message or a good result. They must wait, and work, and make meaning in the space between triumph and tribulation.

Unitarian Universalist musician and theologian Glen Thomas Rideout says that the predominantly white-identified congregations within our liberal faith, "allow ourselves to overdose on the worship of goodness." In so doing, "we lopside our spirits to the point that they feel poisoned by the presence of tragedy . . . we gorge ourselves on this notion of fundamental human goodness without taking a bite of fundamental human inequity."[32]

And so, while the global marginalized still live from one Holy Saturday to another in the presence of a powerful and decidedly non-triumphal *esperanza,* the American liberal religious tradition rides its instinct toward time travel into an eternal expectation of a bright new dawn.

Even in the unavoidable presence of tragedy, we find ourselves clamoring for Eastertide, reaching out for the triumph that once seemed like a given, and scooping up another helping of hopeful optimism to soothe us into believing that we ourselves, acting primarily for ourselves, still have the power to make the arc of history bend toward justice.

Four

Respectable Church People and the Kingdom of God

> They constantly try to escape . . .
> By dreaming of systems so perfect that no one will need to
> be good.
>
> —T.S. Eliot[33]

A few years ago, somewhere near the ten-year mark of my professional ministry, I had finally figured out how the copy machine worked—at least well enough to branch out a bit to other pursuits. Among those was the shared labor of building a broad-based community organizing coalition. As had happened once before, in the early stages of my ministry, my close relationships with colleagues and people of faith from other denominations pieced me together and helped provide context to my calling.

At one point, after hundreds of hours of meetings and research, my colleagues and I organized ourselves smack into the middle of a years-long campaign to build government and corporate reinvestment in local neighborhoods that were hard hit by the 2008 foreclosure crisis. This is what broad-based community organizations do at their very best. With intention and interconnection, they pick fights that matter.

With the backing of our congregations, this little group of widely diverse, multicultural and interfaith leaders were trying to seal the deal on a multimillion-dollar corporate reinvestment fund that would keep hundreds of our congregants and community members in their homes. If we played our cards right, we could make an impact that changed our community in significant and previously unimagined ways.

Through grit, luck, and a great deal of tension, we had managed to score a meeting with top-level executives at one of the most prominent banking institutions in the country—a multinational corporation that had made millions of dollars in our community by pushing high-risk mortgages in low-income neighborhoods.

You know the story. They bet against their own assets and set the people up to fail, leaving whole neighborhoods blighted and cutting yet more people of color off from any way of building generational wealth. Same old, same old. They knew just what they'd done. And we knew just how much power they had.

Our job was to inform the senior vice presidents of this powerful economic institution that their share of the foreclosure reinvestment fund would be something like a hundred million dollars.

While we knew enough to acknowledge that we were power players at the negotiation table, that morning almost all of us were nervous, none more than me.

At our pre-meeting breakfast that morning, we debated and rewrote our opening remarks while one of us spilled coffee on his tie. We were twenty minutes behind schedule before we even got in our cars to leave for the posh corporate boardroom in which we would meet those executive vice presidents in their bespoke suits.

Then, because we live in DC, there was awful traffic. I got us good and lost, rerouting us halfway across downtown before bashfully admitting that I am in fact a god-awful excuse for a driver.

Finally, after tapping a bumper ahead of me more than a couple of times while attempting to parallel park, my colleagues and I burst through the lobby of the massive corporate office building just in time to wipe the sweat from our brows before the handlers of the bigwigs came out of the elevator to escort us up.

We had not eaten much at breakfast and were left alone by these corporate handlers in a conference room that inexplicably had a wide variety of individually wrapped snack cakes prominently on display in the middle of the table. As someone procured and promptly lost the bathroom key, the rest of us shoved said snack cakes into our purses and tried to sit in such a way that the coffee stain on the tie wouldn't show.

If the stakes weren't so high, it would have been hilarious. Though we were leaders of the largest congregations in one of the most politically important jurisdictions in the entire country, though we were accompanied by organizers who had fought for and won power across all sectors of society and trained change agents who knew how to act strategically—still, for a moment, we projected all the confidence of country bumpkins recently arrived in the big city, tasked with asking the very scions of corporate power for a whole lot of cash.

Everyone looked around the room and chuckled a little bit at our discombobulation. We twitched uncomfortably in our posh leather armchairs. All was silent for a moment until my friend Gerry—a rabble-rousing 45-year veteran of the Catholic priesthood, personal friend to Ethel Kennedy, and the only one among us who remained unfazed, looked directly at me and made a life-changing pastoral declaration in his sonorous Irish brogue.

"Ah Nancy," he said, "strange birds roost in the tree of heaven."

And that was that. And hour and a half later we walked out of that place well on our way to a multimillion-dollar investment. Stains and rushing and the whereabouts of the bathroom key notwithstanding, we were exactly the imperfect, engaged, flawed, and finite people who needed to be in that room.

This was true in part because we had worked so hard together to get there, but it was also true because that moment was not the ultimate triumph of a series of escalating successes. In fact, we had failed together more than once before we arrived in that boardroom—over and over again, in fact. By that point, we had been organizing intensively as a multicultural, multiracial, multifaith collective for more than a year, and you don't dive that deeply into important work without lurching back and forth a time or two.

There had been evenings in empty church basements when our plans had fallen apart in the presence of power. There had been strategies that crumbled to dust when our people failed to show up for them. And while we didn't know it that day, there would be moments in the months ahead when those mighty plans would crumble again. We did not always win the day. We were not the heroes of our own story. At least one of us was a truly terrible driver.

But we were the only raw material that the Holy Spirit had to work with in those days. We were the ones committed both to the task at hand and to each other, and there was no one else to engage the dynamics of power except for us—we strange and stumbling birds whom grace itself and the ministry of the progressive church had drawn together.

"Strange birds roost in the kingdom of heaven," my friend had said. That single line, tossed out with such studied yet seemingly casual grace, emerges from the history of the Christian tradition at its very best—a tradition in which strange and stumbling birds like us are repeatedly drawn together for holy work.

Like many rabbis before and after him, Jesus was a man who taught in parables. Everything was a story with him, and most of his parables eventually come around, by hook or by crook, to a description of what is variously transcribed in the Gospel traditions as the kingdom of heaven or the kingdom of God. Within the context of first-century politics in the Levant, the kingdom of heaven wasn't merely an otherworldly paradise, but a countercultural vision of what life might be like if the Jewish people could live out from under the oppressive thumb of the Roman Empire. The kingdom of heaven was the world as it could be, connected to and informed by the world as it really was.

In one of the very best parables in his playbook, Jesus evokes the kingdom of heaven in the image my colleague would later use to pull us out of a state of awkward shame and back into the honest and unglamorous work of effective social change.

In the Gospel of Luke, the bearded one from Galilee says, "The kingdom of heaven is like a mustard seed that a man took and tossed in his garden. It grew and became a tree and the birds of the sky roosted in its branches."

This seems innocuous enough. The parables often do at first glance. A mustard seed is usually understood in popular biblical interpretation to mean something infinitesimally small. Under that simple meaning it would hold that a tiny thing became something huge, and the message of this parable would be so simple as to be a cliché—from humble beginnings grand things might arise.

But anybody who has ever spent a good deal of time in the Near East knows that the mustard plant in Galilee is generally associated with something quite different from mere smallness. The mustard plant, in the context in which this story was first told, would have been thought of as a useful but tenacious weed that, once planted, spreads out and takes over all available space.

As Pliny the Elder wrote around 77 CE in his *Natural History*, "Mustard grows entirely wild, though it is improved by being transplanted; but on the other hand, when it has once been sown it is scarcely possible to get the place free of it, as the seed when it falls germinates at once."[34]

Jesus says that the kingdom of heaven is like a humble shrubbery that a man took and tossed into his garden on purpose, a low-lying plant that somehow grows up into a mighty tree that brushes the sky. It is a dandelion that grows higher than the redwoods.

That image is absurd enough in and of itself, but that's not all—not only is the kingdom of heaven like this massive skyscraper of a shrubbery, but all the birds of the sky in that holy kingdom, all those weird birds who have no place else to go, come to make their home there.

In Jesus' image, the kingdom of heaven is tenacious, ever unfolding, and more than a little bit strange. According to my beloved friends and fellow interfaith organizers, those who make a home within it are odd ducks and outliers.

A tenacious weed shall outgrow them all. And strange birds will roost there. And everything you thought was sacred will be upended by the odd, imperfect things you have always overlooked.

In the end, I like to imagine that we will shelter ourselves not in the branches of mighty oaks, but in the waving fronds of crabgrass. We will build a whole new world not by being grandly at home in the comfort and security of the beautiful places, but by being disarmingly at home in the forgotten ones.

When we sat there, flawed, finite, and weird, late and sweaty and shoving oatmeal cream pies in our purses, it didn't matter if we, the representatives of the progressive church itself, were something less than stately cedars, straight of back and pure of mind. It didn't matter that we weren't perfect and we didn't have it all figured out. Because strange birds roost in the tree of heaven, and our blessedness as leaders and as human beings is found precisely in the moment when our personal inadequacy meets our collective power.

Yet, even though the scriptures themselves call us to thrive in the marginalized imperfections the world disdains, over and over again the progressive and mainline churches, influenced by the brightly polished upper-class modernism that we have already discussed, persisted in imagining themselves and their grand edifices as the center point of respectability in American culture for most of the twentieth century.

It was a curious transubstantiation that morphed the weird, imperfect, broken, and blessed rabble of the early Christian Church into the stately, august, middle-class conservators of American culture that we know today. Inside the movement of that shift, the largely white Protestant churches began to communicate that their sheltering walls were mainly built for those small-time sinners who still basically had their shit together.

To conserve middle-class Eurocentric values, the progressive Protestant churches aligned themselves with respectability instead of strangeness, with privilege instead of complexity, with socioeconomic and racial uniformity instead of the intersections of overlapping identities.

Consequently, the professed and self-understood nature of the people who filled their pews both during and after the modern era continued to be seen as more enlightened, or at least a good bit smarter, than the diverse and differently educated masses who gathered to live and struggle and survive outside of the sanctuary doors.

As I first uneasily observed in seminary when I made my way into the progressive academy—*we were so damn sure of ourselves.*

What we projected along with this sense of surety was an unshakable confidence that we were among the good people—along with a willingness to go only so far in alignment with the authentic pain, struggle, oppression, and experiences of those who refused to perform their own respectability inside the church.

During and after the modern era, we planted our churches like steepled architectural redwoods on expensive real estate and imagined that graceful eagles roosted there at the center of power. We forgot, somehow, that the church was always meant to be scrappy and the strange birds were always meant to make a home there.

The consequences of this turn toward a curated, even highly polished self-expression within the liberal church are not insignificant. Like all the fundamental errors that eat at the heart of liberal utopias past and present, this choice has a price.

At least part of the price the liberal church has paid for a curated and self-assured presentation of respectable identity is the fact that marginalized peoples of various stripes have struggled to be included within the fold, even as we profess the continued expansiveness of our welcome.

The Price of Professed Perfectibility

Back home in southern Indiana, my own grandmother, Dorothy McDonald, was born into chilling poverty just after the turn of the twentieth century.

As is often the case with poor families, we don't have a great deal of recorded information to tell us about her people, except that most of them lived far outside the margins of respectability and were likely impacted by the same depressive tendencies and occasional sparks of instability that continue to crop up among my best beloved even now.

My grandmother's people made their way through life in the same fertile flatlands of Indiana, Illinois, and Kentucky that still feel like home to me. They were descended at least indirectly from the same German and Irish tenant farmers whose well-being could not be fully embraced by the Owenite visionary dream of a perfect society.

My grandma's mother died of tuberculosis before she had the chance to get old. She once told me that her sister committed suicide when her young husband ran off to Chicago with "a floozie." It's not even entirely clear who my grandmother would have considered a father figure—her name seems to have changed midway through her high school yearbooks. The whole situation is murky at best.

Grandma married young and got a job. We have always been nose-to-the-grindstone people in my family, and on that point she was the rule who brokered no exceptions. After her husband died in the prime of his life, Dorothy McDonald finished raising four boys all alone on a waitress's tips and got to work every morning and back home again every night by hitchhiking—for thirty years, in high-heeled shoes. This resulted in bunions so big that in her later years she cut holes in her house shoes to accommodate them.

She treated her bunions like they were old friends who needed a little space to spread out, and she upheld only two unbreakable rules in her house: no motorcycles for anyone, and everyone will graduate high school.

If you didn't break either of those mandates too obviously, pretty much everything else was fair game, though the depth of her disappointment could sometimes be measured in the baleful stare of her deep-set eyes.

I loved my grandmother very deeply. She taught my big sister and me that it was our job to stick it to the fakes and the phoneys of the world in any way we could. She blew raspberries at the fancy people and never forgot her purse, even toward the end of her life when it was filled mostly with damp napkins and lint-covered candies. She considered herself a Christian, though I do not remember ever seeing her pray. During her memorial service, over the platters of fried chicken and chafing dishes of cheesy potato casserole, my dad told me something about my grandmother's relationship to the church that still cuts me to the core.

My father is the youngest of Dorothy's four boys, and he said that when he was small, she had taken the little ones, including him, to Sunday school every week. She dressed them in their best clothes, combed down their cowlicks, and took them over to the little country United Church of Christ sanctuary not far from her rather dumpy but always warm home.

At that point, my dad says, she almost always dropped them off and walked away.

When I met the minister who serves that church today, I was shocked to hear that she had made a financial pledge to that congregation for years, even though she virtually never went inside it. She just dropped the boys off in their good Sunday clothes and left.

Looking back on that time, my dad said he thinks she didn't feel like she fit in there. Furthermore, she didn't like the way the people saw her there—always through the lens of what they perceived to be the tragic circumstances in her life.

My grandmother concluded that the church on the back road in the dusty place she called home wasn't really made for her. Seeing herself through the lens of their perception, she imagined that her story was too tragic and her lifestyle too impoverished for the proper type of company she would have to keep within the walls of the church.

So, she did what she knew to do. She got the boys to church just in time for Sunday school and she came back an hour later, confident that her children at least were normal and upstanding enough to roost in the tree of heaven among God's people, while she herself was not.

It pains me to think that the woman who made me who I am would very likely not feel comfortable among the denizens of the liberal churches I now serve. She would shrink from career-connected, coffee-hour conversation and size up the make and model of still-shiny hybrid cars in the parking lot. All the while she would know herself to be a stranger in the systematically curated middle-class culture all around her.

Like so many people with complex triumphs, stories, and experiences, she was living in a world that the church somehow could not account for, moving in a present reality of struggle and subsistence that was deemed either altogether pitiable or unpleasantly undignified among the proper people of God.

The Shelter of Perception

This lack of perception has plagued the liberal church since before my grandmother's time. What she experienced in that little country United Church of Christ sanctuary is not uncommon in the liberal church today—the lifting up of comfortable respectability over actual relational presence alongside one another in a broken world.

This culture of respectability still weighs heavily today, keeping us focused on all the ways in which a prevailing status quo of Eurocentric middle-class identity is safe and comforting for those of us who have the privilege of perpetuating it.

Rebecca Parker has long been a gentle and insistent voice within liberal Christianity and the Unitarian Universalist tradition as we struggle to articulate an honest hope in painful times. As a minister, she knows the power of perception and the sometimes deadly implications of white liberal inattention.

In her writing, Parker describes traveling with a friend through the midst of a rising rainstorm. Fields stretched out before them, full of standing water. The river over which they drove was coursing so fast they could hear it as they approached. Sandbags lined the low-lying areas and the edges of the water. It looked like there had been a flood, they thought. It looked as if something had happened there, in the world just outside their doors.

Turning down one last road, they saw standing water in the middle of their path. The water was moving, flowing even, and at first they thought this meant it was receding and the way forward would soon enough be clear.

Shielded by their perception of safety, they drove along, carrying an abstract worry for a crisis that surely was impacting other people.

They continued worrying about the impact this dangerous storm was having on others until they fully perceived what was happening all around them.

The water wasn't receding. It was going up. It wasn't the aftermath of a flood they were encountering—it was happening right then. "The water was rising fast," she writes,

> We started to turn the car around [but] the water was rising behind us as well. Suddenly we realized the flood hadn't happened yesterday or last week. It was happening here and now. Dry ground was disappearing fast. We hurriedly clambered out of the car and scrambled to higher ground. Soaked to the bone, we huddled under a fir tree. The cold water of the storm poured down on us, baptizing us into the present—a present from which we had been insulated by both our car and our misjudgments about the country we had been travelling through.[35]

What my grandmother encountered in the 1960s was a church that had come to conceive of itself as a privileged shelter from the real events, real sufferings, and real risks of people's lives. It was a place where actual pain, actual suffering, and even the no-fault tragedies of a poor woman's life could not fit into the narrative the people told about themselves.

It was a place where decent, struggling people performed their well-being for each other so effectively that one who lived just a little more obviously at the margins of wealth and power could not find a home among them.

Every Sunday morning I stand before the congregation as the sum of my identities, experiences, misjudgments, and limitations of perception. These are served up to the people alongside whatever flashes of wisdom I can muster.

Because it is both obvious and often unremarked upon, I also stand before my congregation as a white woman of some economic freedom who is capable—when I choose—of driving right through the middle of a flood of injustice all the while imagining that every-thing is really just fine.

If I am not careful, I can subtly or overtly proclaim such percep-tions of safety from the chancel on Sunday morning. If we are not aware, our respectable and mostly white communities can unwit-tingly but loudly proclaim such comfortable assertions as well.

Somewhere there is a woman dropping off her kids in the Sun-day school wing of a good liberal church before heading out to the parking lot to catch the bus and ride away. Somewhere there is a soul just waiting to be welcomed in, past the performance of respectabili-ty and into a community where the people will finally admit that the waters of injustice are rising to threaten us all together.

Impinging on Our Previously Scheduled Lives

The prophet Isaiah once said that those who are asleep to the world will constantly listen without understanding and see without per-ceiving. He preached that they would move through the astonishing times given unto them, unable to absorb the danger, the reality, or the mission inherent in the moment.

In reflecting on her perception of the flood, Parker also wrote that to be white in America "is to travel ensconced in a secure vehicle." It is, she said, "to see signs of what is happening in the world outside your compartment and not realize that these signs have any contem-porary meaning. It is to misjudge your location, and believe you are uninvolved and unaffected by what is happening in the world."[36]

If we allow ourselves to assume that the inundation of poverty, patriarchy, xenophobia, and white supremacy isn't happening but has already happened in some former time or some other place, the respectable people of the liberal church can resume our previously scheduled lives.

In my grandmother's time, those previously scheduled lives in-cluded gender norms that tied a woman's worth to the continued presence of a fine, upstanding husband. They included finely pressed shirtwaists, a car to drive to church, and children who didn't have dirt underneath their nails. In short, the previously scheduled lives the good church people professed to live did not include many of the core aspects of her identity, her struggle, or her triumph.

Today, the previously scheduled lives of the denizens of the liberal church are not fully rid of the specter of patriarchal submission. People still ask me, the senior minister of a large and successful liberal church, if I actually wrote the text of my own sermons. After all, they imply, while looking me over for a beat too long, I'm just a girl. Clearly someone who *looks more like a minister* has helped me.

Today, the previously scheduled lives of the respectable church people include a comfortable state of half-baked race consciousness where we don't see race and consequently don't particularly want to talk about race in church at all.

This previously scheduled comfort also means that we don't need to make hiring decisions that preference diversity because we're only looking for "the best person for the job." It means we don't have to worry about the survival of young Black men because the ones who died at the end of a gun weren't caught up in a flood of continued injustice but instead were snatched away by happenstance and unfortunate but isolated mistakes.

The previously scheduled lives of the good church people are contrived in such a way that we are routinely justified in our efforts to disengage, to rationalize, and to retreat.

Being white, privileged, and sheltered behind the walls of progressive institutions doesn't mean being on the wrong side of history. It doesn't mean those in the liberal church who hold those identities are obligated to endless guilt-ridden self-flagellation about our ancestors' place in the story, nor does it mean we are called to banal and inchoate repentance for the fact that the playing field still isn't level.

What it means, on a practical level, is that the liberal church is still capable of repeatedly making the choice to circle the wagons of community life around a conservator's vision of the status quo. We can continue to draw the shape of the church so narrowly that those who are at risk of either tragedy or harder-earned triumph need not knock on the door. Or we can choose to live a different way. Both choices are within our capacity, and both choices are freely extended to us over and over again.

My grandmother thought that this tree of heaven that rooted itself in the church was only for people who had things figured out and could afford to meet each other at the intersection of their shared middle-class values. She thought that a seemingly endless projection of confidence in one's own powers was a required precondition for full participation in the church.

I wonder what it would take to stop imagining the progressive churches as mighty cedars fit to serve as houses for respectability and instead reframe our self-understanding as something more akin to the kingdom of God here on earth—a place where we welcome all the strange birds back home, every one of us struggling, seeking, wondering, and waiting as we drive through the storm together.

I suspect it would require us to take apart our perception of safety as well as our perception of power. I suspect that it would require all of us to cultivate a willingness to claim both our capacity to harm one another and the astonishing depth of our dependence on one another—before it is too late.

Five

The Will to Power and the Power of Mutuality

The wisdom of the Desert Fathers includes the wisdom that the hardest spiritual work in the world is to love the neighbor as the self—to encounter another human being not as someone you can use, change, fix, help, save, enroll, convince, or control, but simply as someone who can spring you from the prison of yourself, if you will allow it. All you have to do is recognize another you "out there"—your other self in the world—for whom you may care as instinctively as you care for yourself. To become that person, even for a moment, is to understand what it means to die to yourself. This can be as frightening as it is liberating. It may be the only real spiritual discipline there is.

—Barbara Brown Taylor[37]

Throughout the modern era and beyond, the liberal branches of the American church have been steadily engaged in a grand theological project of reforming the reputation of human nature.

Since even before the modern era, a reformed doctrine of human nature in relationship to the holy (theological anthropology, if you will allow me some seminary words) has been steadily on the rise. In response to the depravity preached by conservative and evangelical traditions, progressive American Protestants have long sought to lift up the almost endless reach of enlightened human possibility.

This uplifting of human nature is certainly a worthwhile theological project. Among other things, it has helped to knit back together the ideological separation of body and spirit, reminding us that our physical form isn't evidence of our fallenness. It's offered us eager glimpses of our deep responsibility to pair our abundant potential with wisdom. It's given us the chance to begin our spiritual journeys from an assumption of original blessing.

And yet, even this central doctrine of basic human goodness, left unchecked and unexamined, can be used as a clever mechanism to let optimistic progressive people off the hook for our less benevolent proclivities. The high theological anthropology we have built in the liberal church over succeeding generations has sometimes provided reinforcement for a familiar privileged assurance of our own innate goodness. It is part of why we are so darn sure of ourselves.

In his widely acclaimed 1941 essay, "The Changing Reputation of Human Nature," James Luther Adams pivots from his important critique of progressivist history to a deep and thoughtful analysis of the liberal church's various doctrines of human nature. He offers a finely crafted takedown of the shiny, distracting vision of human perfectibility that continues to draw our collective attention today.

Adams argues that in both the classical Greek tragedies and the scriptures of the Christian tradition, there exists "an awareness of an ontologically grounded tendency in humanity toward rebellion, perversion, and self-destruction."[38] Along with his fellow liberal Christians, he concedes that the incarnated example of Christ's life was made to triumph over this innate tendency toward self-destruction, but he also asserts that the whole human situation remains essentially tragic. No matter what Jesus did or didn't do to absolve us, we've still got some significant work to do on ourselves.

This is not to say that the human condition is essentially or inherently debased in Adams's theology. He certainly doesn't want progressives in the mid-twentieth century to take up some sort of dour, self-flagellating return to Calvinist doctrines of election and damnation. He just wants us to take our death-dealing tendencies seriously for a change, instead of barreling through them on the way to a brighter hopey-changey vision of our own capacities. The tragic dimension of our nature is part of our essential being, but certainly not the whole of it, and the tendency toward destruction within ourselves can be mitigated more fully if we addressed it during our shared community life.

Adams says that by the middle of the twentieth century, the rationalistic branches of the Protestant church had steadily moved away not only from a doctrine of Calvinist debasement, but from any authentic acknowledgment of the tragic dimension of human nature altogether. Having done so, the liberal church aligned itself with a false doctrine of human perfectibility that was just as misguided as the false doctrine of human brokenness the fire and brimstone prophets liked to declare.

We came by this high-vaunted doctrine of human nature through good old-fashioned theological means. As always, we inherited our big ideas from other big thinkers who thought big thoughts before.

Adams argues that sometime after the Middle Ages, heterodox Christian thinkers began to imagine that there existed a "pre-established harmony" in the universe. This was so powerful that it could maintain fundamental unity and unidirectional movement among people and things, even amid seeming diversity. This harmony drew human creatures inevitably toward itself. Basically, it taught that all things, including us, were headed in the right direction.

Adams claims that this faith in the eventual harmonious unity of all things contributed to the development of an unrealistic view of human nature within American religious liberalism. It led us to develop a doctrine of our own eventual attainment of moral perfection. In his words,

> Because of the pre-established harmony, separative individualism was given a divine sanction, and the modern Liberal's over-optimism about human nature, its possibilities for growth, and its progressive and ultimate perfectibility was born.[39]

If we conceived of creation as an inherently harmonious whole, and reminded ourselves for hundreds of years that each of us was one perfectly made part of a greater perfectly made whole—it wasn't such a difficult leap to assume that someday we might find ourselves in perfect harmony with the one that did all the creating in the first place. Basically, we might just become one with God in the end.

And so, among the more reformist branches of the ever-diversifying tree of American religion, nineteenth-century preachers began to teach that the image of God was manifested in the world through the living example of the morally and spiritually ideal human being. There was more than enough grist for that theological mill to be found in the history of the Christian tradition.

As far back as the fourth century, the Cappadocian Monk Gregory of Nyssa argued that humans alone among all other beings were created in the image of God. More than a millennium later, American liberalism began to teach that the inherent presence of this *imago dei,* or image of God, meant that all we needed to do to come into perfect unity with the almighty itself was to live lives of perpetual moral growth and spiritual advancement. Certain strands of theological thinking taught that perpetual growth and advancement were in fact what God had in mind for us all along.

In the fourth century, when St. Augustine was the brightest theological light on the block, a British ascetic named Pelagius opposed his doctrine of original sin by arguing that God would not task human beings with becoming perfectly moral creatures unless it was truly possible for them to do just that.

In this way, the distinct possibility of human perfection got all wrapped up with God's will in our creation. Why would God hold us to a standard we could never meet? The followers of Pelagius thought that sounded like a weird kind of torture. In time, some branches of the liberal tradition came to agree with him. Our forebears were simply not willing to lay that kind of meanness in the lap of God.

In American religion, it was the Universalists who proclaimed that none of us was going to hell, at least not permanently. And while universalism is plenty hip in progressive Christian circles now, in the nineteenth century it was a bold and risky thing to claim that God's other name was "love."

In fact, to some within the nineteenth- and twentieth-century liberal church, the purpose of life was to love so fully, so richly, that we could become like God. To them, the indwelling of the *imago dei* in the human creature made such motions toward perfection possible. The image of God was within us. Through our efforts, and God's grace, we could bring it out, and when we saw it in one another, we could justifiably celebrate our progress, perhaps while singing rousing songs of moral uplift.

And yet, that rousing and optimistic faith the American Universalists sacrificed for over the course of generations has too frequently been only halfway interpreted and partially shared. We've often told it as a story that is *all about us*—about the fundamental goodness and inevitable progress of human beings. We've made this essential Universalist component of our progressive theological legacy a testament to our own inherent goodness. We've neglected to give credit where credit is due.

On closer examination, we see that the full story is less about how great we are and more about how great God is. It's not a doctrine of our own fundamental goodness, but a story about the fundamental greatness of a God who will not let us go, no matter how stumbling and befuddled we often are.

The great Universalist theologian Hosea Ballou made a powerful impact on nineteenth-century progressive religion, all without ever slipping into the presupposition that human beings were so darn awesome. In fact, along with many other early American Universalists, he never centered his theology of salvation on humankind at all.

Instead of focusing on how pure and perfect people were, Ballou taught that sin was finite while God was infinite. Since God's omnipotence and infinite benevolence was way, way vaster than all our shortcomings, God could work through the finite sin of the human condition for the realization of the greater good. Basically, God could work with whatever raw materials He was given to work with, even when those materials were imperfect, slightly dumpy, and occasionally weird—like us.

In the Universalist good news, everything we do, both for good and ill, is finite and limited, while everything God does is infinite and complete. The great Universalists who preached universalism when universalism wasn't cool never assumed that human beings' intentions could be pure and unblemished. They simply believed that God's love was more powerful than our deadlier proclivities.

In fact, they taught that it is our finite and ever-shifting nature that differentiates us from the divine in the first place. There's a reason human beings aren't gods, and it's got something to do with the fact that we are not now, never have been, and never will be perfect.

Imago Dei: When the Image of God Looks Like an Old White Man

It's probably fair to say that the modernist twentieth-century project of rehabilitating human nature didn't draw its primary ideological power from nineteenth-century Universalists. That oomph came, more directly, from nineteenth-century secular progressives like Robert Owen and the white male denizens of powerful progressive Congregationalist and Unitarian pulpits around the country.

This whole idea of human beings as reflective of the image of God was articulated most clearly by the famous forefather of American Unitarianism, William Ellery Channing. In his doctrine of human nature, the Godly essence deeply embedded in the human soul was reflected in our capacities for reason, imagination, moral conscience, and aesthetic appreciation.

He taught that sin could obscure our ability to reflect this inherent image of God in our lives, as could experiences of human suffering. Our messy emotional baggage and pain occlude the clear reflection of God. And so, he figured, all our baggage ought to be gotten out of the way if we are going to go about manifesting God's image more fully in the world.

To Channing, the inherent greatness of the soul was hidden from view by ignorance, suffering, and pain. The answer to all this was what he called self-culture: the work of freeing up the Godly image inherent in each human soul. Self-culture was a way of nurturing one's inherent greatness of soul through advanced learning, prayerful practice, and acts of mercy. Along with many others, Channing believed that creating opportunities for this refined moral cultivation was the primary work of the liberal church in the world.

It was exactly the kind of leisurely, subdued, and perfectly respectable activity that the moneyed classes could engage in on a Sunday afternoon. Which worked out well for the respectable, educated, moneyed merchant class of worshippers who attended Channing's church. They had time for all that stuff.

Since certain classes of people were free to study and serve in the ways commonly uplifted in the practice of self-culture, the very most cultivated people, reflecting most clearly the image of God, tended to be the least oppressed, the least poor, and the least at risk of bodily harm.

Reflecting about a century later this period in American religious history, James Luther Adams said that this push toward cultivated self-culture became the cultural centerpiece of the liberal church. For some in the modernist era, this self-culture was the whole point of religion itself, and the fact that it was largely inaccessible to anyone beyond a narrow band of privileged individuals registered with varying degrees of seriousness and dismissal.

After World War II, Adams could not content himself with the remaining dregs of this class-bound and carefully studied progressive over-optimism. Like the contemporary ecologists, liberation theologians, and social theorists we considered in the previous chapter, he too saw the progress of humanity onward and upward forever as a sham that would ultimately leave religious liberals unable to relate meaningfully to those who come face to face with the deadlier manifestations of oppression.

Adams writes that history is much like human nature in that both contain a fundamentally tragic dimension. History is and has always been "a theater of conflict in which the tensions between the will to mutuality and the will to power appear in their most subtle and perverse forms. In short, history is tragic."[40]

It is tragic not just because of the nature of history itself, but because of the nature of humankind and the opposing wills that govern it. To him, these wills are always at work in the human heart. They are what pull us toward self-destruction or interconnection, and he called them, respectively, the will to power and the will to mutuality. In the story Adams tells about our nature, it is not a genteel process of respectable self-culture that forms the basis of a strong moral character, but a constant visceral battle between these wills.

Since he believed the selfish and sometimes death-dealing component of our inner state is just as real as the equally commanding will to mutuality, he confronted the optimistic liberal religious tradition by articulating a realistic doctrine of human nature free from self-deception and hide-bound self-congratulation. We don't need more faith in our capacity to lift ourselves up by our proverbial bootstraps, but a renewed commitment to *conversion* in the liberal church—a wholesale turning away from the will to personally accumulated power and toward the will to mutuality.

If we do not allow ourselves to be converted both individually and collectively toward the will to mutuality, Adams argues that liberal religion will continue to center itself around the experiences and expectations of people of privilege. This results in a system of exclusion that draws the beloved community squarely along lines dictated by patriarchal, heteronormative, racist, and classist structures of power.

Abstract vs. Immediate Proximity

The great Episcopal and Catholic theologian John Henry Newman once said that religion must expresses itself in particular acts. There is no religion in general; it doesn't exist as a concept. It is made real only through the tangible social forms that it takes and the relationships in which it is enacted.

Thus, a genuine faith can never manifest primarily as a commitment to an abstract and unrealized notion. The religious value that exists only in the abstract is not a religious value at all, but a notional leaning that, in and of itself, does nothing to affect the healing of the world or any salvific enterprise within it.

James Luther Adams calls this tendency toward abstraction within liberal religion a kind of "angelism" that concerns itself primarily with non-corporeal things and an obsession with ideas and concepts far outside of the muck and muddle of the human experience. This stands in the way of our conversion to a truly collective will to mutuality.

To defeat this angelism, he writes, is "to become personally acquainted with the actual conditions, with the people around us, and especially with those who are suffering. Then only does deep speak to deep."[41]

When deep speaks to deep, we are confronted with our own desire to give and receive love. When we become personally acquainted with the lives, stories, sufferings, and hopes of those around us, we are morally transformed not by ideals, but by actual experiences of compassion and conviction. We are not converted to the will-to-mutuality by our intelligence or our learning or our inherent motions toward perfection, but by the power and possibility that comes with authentic human relationship.

This is the work that activist, lawyer, and educator Bryan Stevenson repeatedly calls privileged people of goodwill across the secular and religious spectrum to do. He travels the country exhorting everyone he encounters, especially those nearest the centers of power, to "get proximate" to the multifaceted and complex experience of those who live with unequal opportunity. With faithfulness in the human will toward mutuality, Stevenson believes that "if you are willing to get closer to people who are suffering, you will find the power to change the world."[42]

Yet so many activists find that the liberal church lacks a deep and vulnerable willingness to get close to the suffering of their own people and to the authentic struggles of others outside the church's doors. It is a yearning expressed by liberal religious leaders of color that often goes unmet in their own denominational homes.

Our battles cannot be fought merely by putting the church in relationship to the abstract concept of injustice and the broad idea of reform. Instead, the power to change the world can be gained by relating with humility and grace to the actual people calling out for a more survivable world—even and especially when they call out from the next pew over on Sunday morning.

The power and possibility of liberal religion cannot be realized in the learned man's quiet study. It can only be realized in the circumstances of the relationships we are willing to cultivate. There is no religion in the abstract. And there is no will to mutuality in isolation.

My colleague Glen Thomas Rideout says that the holy moment when change becomes possible arises when we go from professing the abstract notion of our values to extending some actual modicum of acknowledgment of the lived experience of those who suffer at the hands of injustice.

He says that acknowledgment in all its forms is one of the more profound things we can experience. It is, to him, "the fundamental human impulse to say hello to something real." A conversion from fetishized sympathy to genuine acknowledgment pulls us out of the limits of our own perception and into an honest exchange of meaning.

Without this deep-seated conversion experience, Rideout says that any liberal religious tradition that continues to center maleness, whiteness, and wealth has "fooled ourselves into thinking we're actually being empathic to the oppression of Black people when in point of fact we get just close enough to watch it like a car accident."[43]

The work of grappling with white supremacy, patriarchy, and oppression both inside and outside our churches stands not as another opportunity for fetishized sympathy, but as an invitation to exactly the kind of conversion Adams once hoped for.

Only a thoroughgoing invocation of the will to mutuality has the potential to remake the respectable church people as allies and accomplices for liberation. Of course, this remaking by actual proximity and mutual care is dangerous and demanding stuff. It does not always happen inside the life of the church, and it is made possible not despite, but because of, its uncomfortable, difficult, and outright risky implications.

After all, to be transformed and converted, we must let something go. And the cool distance of middle-class reserve that Adams called us out on fifty years ago is a safe and comfortable stance amid society's turmoil. It is also a safe and comfortable place to stand while we continue to offer ourselves unflappable assurances of our own benevolence.

It is so much easier to perceive the building of a just society as a project of benevolent paternalism visited upon others through a divinely ordained charitable instinct than to understand how the absence of a just society kills all of us—if not by bullets, then by a thousand tiny cuts to the integrity of our own souls.

It is easy to imagine that the work of the church is to cultivate our own souls so that we might bind up what is broken among other people. It is so much harder to acknowledge what is and has always been broken within ourselves.

Six

We Are Not Going to Get This Right

Now is the time to resist the slightest extension in the boundaries of what is right and just. Now is the time to speak up and to wear as a badge of honor the opprobrium of bigots. Now is the time to confront the weak core at the heart of America's addiction to optimism; it allows too little room for resilience, and too much for fragility.

—Chimamanda Ngozi Adichi[44]

"This is not a game. We are not going to win." Recently I heard myself saying those words to myself and leaders in the Racial Justice Task Force at the congregation I serve. Collectively, we are just about the best that the liberal church has to offer. Our racial justice leaders come from different backgrounds and different generations. We are learning and struggling at the intersections of class, race, gender, and ethnicity. We are multiracial (though still predominantly white), we are committed, and we are steadily advancing both in our own consciousness and our capacity to combat the injustice of the world. And still, even knowing that we are assembled and self-selected as the people called to bring one liberal church closer to living out its own values, we have to be reminded that the way forward sure isn't straight.

To the very best architects of an anti-oppressive future my congregation has to offer, I found myself declaring, "Nothing in the work of dismantling racism and opposing white supremacy is inherently doable, and nothing that you, or any of us bring into this work will ultimately result in what you might perceive to be a perfect outcome, especially one so gloriously 'successful' that people of color among us will line up to give the white people among us gold stars for all of our efforts."

We are not going to win.

Nothing we do will be perfect. And it will not always, or even very often, feel good to be in the trenches of the fight to decenter white normative culture in our congregations and in the world.

Most of the time when the work is at its most essential, you will not personally be having a great deal of fun. It will break you open if you're paying attention, and your heartbreak will not always be directed "out there," but sometimes right at home, into the very deepest recesses of your soul, where you and I and all of us will come to the dawning realization that we are not now and have never been innocent or perfect or pure.

We are not going to have a perfect strategy.

And the strategy we ultimately follow cannot be a strategy that the white people among us, speaking with the authority we have come to expect in the white-centered institutions we have contrived to build, can set for ourselves.

We are going to stay in it, even when it's hard. For as long as we can, to the extent that our hearts can bear, we are going to stay in it together.

I preach some version of those words repeatedly—not just to the best, most loving, and the most broken-open leaders in my congregation, but also to myself.

I must preach these words like a little litany every time I gather in spaces that are not mine to control, every time I choose to let myself feel the discomfort of my own confusion, every time I am called in and called out for the limits of my own perception.

You are not going to win at this, I remind myself in silent moments. You are not going to get an A+ at allyship. You are not going to go on in one endless motion toward perfection to build the liberal church into an anti-oppressive entity that chooses not to center whiteness. You are not going to get it right, not even close.

It is a litany that I have never stopped needing to hear, because the counter-voice has been so deeply ingrained in our tradition that I hear it too. Underneath the will to mutuality, there is a will to perfection, a will to be personally justified, a will to be effective, and, in the end, through all of our carefully calibrated strategies, a will to win the game that was never meant to be a game at all.

There is an idolatry of expectation that drives us in the liberal churches to imagine that the dismantling of oppression was ever achievable through the limited mechanism of our own personal efforts. Only hubris tells us that social change can be articulated on a spreadsheet and our anti-oppressive credentials can be listed on a flyer.

Part of the reason that we in the liberal church need to preach such humble litanies repeatedly is that this historically high theological anthropology of ours has set us up. Across racial and ethnic spectrums within the church, it has constructed an expectation that we are not only to perform our middle-class, have-our-shit-together perfectibility for one other, but that we will be transmogrified by our own performance into actual morally perfect people.

Liberal religious people not only tend to believe that we are called to perfection, but we also believe that we are already basically perfect, already basically converted, and already basically blessed. At times, we like to imagine these things without allowing for further conversions that might impinge on our freedom to be exactly as we already are and to do exactly what we have been doing all along.

This is especially true for the white liberals among us. Thus, the moment that the supposed ontological goodness of those same responsible white liberals is called into question by voices at the margins of congregational or societal power, a form of guilt arises that can be all but paralyzing.

Speaking from my own social, racial, and ethnic location, I can acknowledge that white people in predominantly white churches generally don't like to play games that we cannot win. We don't like to follow strategies that we did not set. We don't like to enter vulnerably into work at which we will not definitively succeed. As white leaders in the liberal church, our historic theology and lived experience of privilege have doubly conditioned us to these tendencies, and it too often results in our retreat into defensiveness or resignation.

However committed we may be to share liberation, white liberal church people too often fall back on the middle-class comforts of our privilege at the first lived experience of failure. Because we have been taught that we were meant to be perfect, our lack of perfection brings deep fragility to both our spiritual lives and our partnerships for justice.

Not Necessarily Certain

Over and over again, when liberal congregations engage in anti-oppressive and anti-racist work, leaders are met with the same exasperatingly familiar responses. Those with historically granted privileged identities ask why it is that they must be "made to feel" so guilty for the trauma visited upon people of color. They lament the ways in which racial justice work distracts from the personal, spiritual, and individual soul food they have come to expect from congregational life. They question if there is a place for them in a congregation that continues to challenge basic assumptions about their own inherent responsibility and goodness.

As a pastor, I can't ignore the fear, discomfort, and even alienation that is voiced by the people I am called to serve. I also can't put myself in a place of remote and self-righteous dismissal when I encounter it. The transformation of institutions, theologies, and self-understanding is profoundly difficult. It proceeds at the pace at which trust is built, and not faster. It is the work of ministry, and it is deeply and profoundly pastoral in nature. After all, transformation is scary, and none of us is entirely sure how we'll get to the kingdom once we've pointed our steps in its direction.

Like the people I love and serve, I'm not always so sure of where we're headed, especially when the center of liberal religion finally moves away from our long-standing fealty to whiteness and respectability. I am not even necessarily certain what the next steps are for my own congregation, which has entrusted me to lead alongside them through this transition. I do not have a ten-point plan.

We can be both broken and called forth. We can only be converted from what we have been if we are also loving enough to bless every single flawed but humane thing that went into building our capacity for that conversion—including our periods of resistance and the occasional descent into our fears.

After all, we don't have to be perfect. We don't have to be God's own image to be worthy of continuing the work, and we don't have to be paragons of fearless virtue to deserve the simple grace of second chances.

Flawed people can be afraid; they can fail and try again. People of privilege aren't broken irreparably by that privilege. The will to personal power doesn't negate the will to mutuality. There is always another chance and a different story to tell about who we think we're meant to be in this beautiful and tragic world.

Theological Anthropology for the Faithful and the Faithless

There is a reimagining of progressive theological anthropology that is already well under way, both inside and outside of the liberal churches. It spans the spectrum of theistic and atheistic worldviews and picks up where most of our misguided expectations of perfection leave off. The work behind that reimagining is being done by diverse leaders from multiple theological viewpoints, and while it does not assume innate goodness on the part of human beings, it makes a few alternate assumptions.

One of the most important of those assumptions is the idea that we human beings do in fact have a great deal of agency. We can make choices. And the choices we make, like the stories we tell, make us. If we build from this framework, human beings are not likened unto angels or demons, but created repeatedly by the exercise of our own agency and the relationships that constrain and define our lives.

An emerging theological anthropology for the liberal church can also be in conversation with various theologies and philosophies about the exact measure of this agency. How free are we, really? How independent are our choices? What is the measure of our dependence on sources outside of our individual selves?

If we are going to rebuild a doctrine of human nature that allows for brokenness while also regularly experiencing conversion toward a will to mutuality, we must acknowledge that the converse will to power does not necessarily emerge from any force outside of our own human agency and experience. There are no devils here. No demon forces our hand.

Process theologian Marjorie Hewitt Suchocki writes that the capacity to violence itself is built into our species as an extension of our struggle for survival. In her thinking, the pull away from mutuality and toward self-centeredness is partly formed by a basic biological will to make it through another day.

The morally neutral manifestations of this will are evidenced most acutely in the lives of those whose survival is regularly called into question, especially by an oppressive state or system of genocidal destruction.[45]

It stands to reason that the will to survive is not, in and of itself, an expression of evil or evidence of an inherently corruptible nature. It is an expression of basic human need that can be stated in either purely scientific or largely theological terms. We don't want to be destroyed. We do violent things to stay alive.

To Suchoki, however, the turn from a morally neutral response to a threat and toward a morally damaging choice to create danger for others has everything to do with our human freedom. This turn comes when humanity's tendency toward violence is expressed as an unnecessary and altogether avoidable will to consolidate greater power and greater autonomy for the individual person or the tribe.

When the violence innate in the biology of being human is expressed as a choice that has nothing to do with our own survival, Suchoki is bold enough to name it for what it is—a sin.[46]

In this way, human beings do not fall from grace, but to violence.

Pulling from a tradition of feminist and womanist scholars before her, Unitarian Universalist minister Molly Housh Gordon has defined sin as an individual or collective behavior that denies or violates our connection with other humans, other creatures, or our planet. A sin, she says, is "an action that is not 'in touch' . . . with our mutual relationship to other beings and with the whole."[47]

Gordon explains that sin is a process of "domination or exercise of control" that denies the lived experience and unique identity of another human being. It is a falling away from the greater whole, a willful choice to engage with the powers that destroy rather than the mutuality that sustains.

While Gordon does not define this interconnected network in expressly theistic terms, her sense of mutual dependency on a broader sphere of relationship puts us into contact with something so much larger than our individual selves. Nothing we do is accomplished in a vacuum, and the "entanglement" of the choices presented to each human soul every day reminds us of both the extent of our freedom and the reality of our interconnection.

It follows that, for both theists and nontheists alike, a renewed theological anthropology for liberal religion does not necessitate a view of the individual human soul as debased and/or powerless before the corrupting forces of some external demonic voice. It also does not invite us to return to a pattern of nineteenth-century, male-centered self-culture in which the refined soul remakes himself in the studied image of a patriarchal God. That's not the kind of God we're looking for.

If it is authentically grounded in love and accountability, our relationship to God in the liberal church is not supposed to be simple. It demands something of us. It compels us to find new courage. Anyone who has ever been in love can profess that it is not generally so cozy a thing. Love—of oneself, of one another, or of God—is bold, heartbreaking, and more than a little scary.

If God's name is love, then God compels us to resist the fall to sinful violence by pushing back with muscular resolve against the social structures that confine our capacity to care. A universalist God for a tragic era is not a gauzy, hymn-singing force of personal devotion that draws us endlessly toward itself, but a fierce and compelling power that grips us by the collar amid our rebellious descent and calls us to choose the will to mutuality all over again, even when that choice is so risky that it could utterly remake us.

On the other side of the theological spectrum, scholar Anthony B. Pinn is doing some of the most compelling nontheistic humanist theology today. To him, the starting place for a renewed theological anthropology is obviously not in the reflection of God's image through the created person. Instead, it is in the profound embodied aesthetic of the human experience.

He says that the deepest truths about human nature cannot be known through either sacred texts or the stories extrapolated from those texts. Rather, what can be known of our true nature is encountered through science and in "the development of culturally bound discourse" in relationship to the stories, the experiences, and the knowledge of others. In his view, there is no human being that is not inside of a body, responding to other bodies, and moving together in mutuality. He writes,

> Humans, as embodied selves with will, are flawed, but this does not constitute the grounds for a basic need for ontological reconstruction. . . . The goal of this theological anthropology is to speak of humans in ways that not only affirm perceptions of experience, but also change the ways in which particular categories of embodied selves (e.g., African American embodied selves) are viewed and processed.[48]

In his nontheistic approach, Pinn does not say that the human condition is inherently tragic. He teaches that we are inherently embodied, and that bodies come with limitations.

The ways we view and engage with the various categories of those fragile, beautiful, sensuous, and breakable human bodies constitute the mechanisms of either inclusion or destruction. Mutuality is a given. Perfection is nonsense. And so, the only motions we can choose are motions toward mutual inclusion or mutual destruction.

Since significant human agency underlies both theistic and non-theistic approaches to an emerging theological anthropology, we are the choosers. And our choices are conditioned by the relationships that define us—relationships between bodies, between cultures, and between ourselves and the divine.

Since we are the choosers, we must become aware of both our power and our culpability in the conversion toward mutuality that will make the future survivable for us all. We are indeed powerful. And we are interconnected. And we are responsible for our own damn choices, including the ones that cause deep harm. If liberal religion is to step into a future of engaged, anti-oppressive work, we will be called to serve not only because others are broken or the system is broken, but because, as Bryan Stevenson says, "I am broken too."

> I do what I do because I am broken too, and the truth is that if you get proximate, if you change narratives, if you are required to stay hopeful, if you do uncomfortable things, it will break you.
>
> But I also realized . . . that there is a power in brokenness. It is the broken among us who can teach us the way compassion works. It is the broken who understand the power of mercy. It is the broken who understand the power of justice. It is the broken that yearn for redemption. It is the broken who yearn for reconciliation. It is the broken who need to teach us how we love despite our brokenness. And it's in brokenness that I realized I'm not just fighting for the condemned. I'm fighting for myself.[49]

Seven

Access to Atonement

Perfection straineth out the quality of mercy.
—Kilian McDonnell[50]

When I was a teenager in the shadow of the dead utopias, I was generally a pretty good kid. I wasn't anybody's hero or anybody's villain. I was decent enough, usually even-keeled, and jointly capable of a solid presentation of respectability and an above-the-bar level of basic human kindness. I did just fine. Doggone it, people liked me.

And yet, the defining characteristic of my adolescent psyche was a polarized self-image that tugged at me in and through the framework of my faith. I was one of those many young people who somehow managed to demand a great deal of ourselves while simultaneously beating up on ourselves for being so utterly inadequate.

For most of my formative years, I swung like a pendulum from believing I should be capable of great feats of Channing-style self-culture to believing I was much too small, too selfish, and too weak to do much of anything.

In the synapses of my altogether neuro-typical, cliché-riddled, adolescent brain, I imagined myself to be either a shining star or a profound failure. To my mind, there was very little middle ground.

When I was nineteen, still in the midst of all of this, I spent some time in a vocational discernment program among the Dominican Sisters of Nashville, Tennessee. Among other things, I was discerning whether or not I had a call to a formal profession within the Catholic

91

sisterhood. Perhaps more importantly, I also was trying to figure out how to cultivate a more authentic and less polarized spiritual life.

I was trying, though I could not have articulated it then, to get off the pendulum between the precipice of unreasonably high expectations and the doldrums of stultifying self-pity. Somehow stepping out of the everyday demands of young adulthood and into the sheltering walls of the St. Cecilia Motherhouse seemed like just the pause that I needed to get myself sorted out.

During our time among the Dominicans, we vocational discernment students were keenly observed by the novice mistress and her small group of partially wimpled assistants. These newly professed sisters didn't wear the full habit yet. They were only partway in, standing in the liminal place after first profession and before final vows.

As such, they were more equipped to meet us where we were. Where we were, of course, was primarily out there—in the world— steeped head to toe in the swirling movement of our lives. When they observed us, the sisters were watching how we interacted with each other and how our spiritual lives were manifested in our personal choices. They had a whole lot to watch. And it turned out that all this careful attention was going somewhere. At the end of the first week, having done this quiet and unobtrusive watching for hours each day, the novice sisters would assign each vocational student a single word that would be the object of our meditation and prayer for the remainder of our time together.

We ate in silence while meditating on that single word. We walked the orchard on the grounds while meditating on that single word. We even played some rousing games of soccer, the fully professed sisters somehow never tripping over their habits, while somewhere in the deep places beneath our hearts we continued to meditate on that single word.

Before the words were dished out and the assignments given, I spent much of my time in conversation with the sisters openly confessing every single one of my prodigious faults. There was a kind of catharsis in getting that inadequacy off my chest. I didn't have to pretend I had it all together. And so, I proclaimed to all who would listen the unavoidable fact of my smallness of heart, the truth of my sometimes shocking (to me, anyway) weaknesses, and my ever-present fear that I was not enough.

Given all that apologetic professing and cathartic barfing-up of self-doubt, I thought for certain that my lesson for prayer and meditation would have something to do with strength, with bucking up, with hard work and self-improvement. Clearly, these people could not fail to see how much I needed to be whipped into shape, and clearly they would offer me courage for the journey of my own moral cultivation. Like I said, I was a pretty good kid. I was ready for the challenge.

At the end of that first week, we gathered together in an age-old rite of passage, ready to receive the one-word encapsulation of the work that lay before us. In order to receive our word, we went forward one at a time to stand before the Sisters. As you might imagine, we did so with as much gravity and trepidation as a bunch of first-formers at Hogwarts approaching the sorting hat.

One woman before me was given the word *courage*. She came back to her seat knowing that her task was to be braver than she had been before. Another received *silence* and knew that there was quiet truth between and beneath all the words she was constantly speaking. Another got *reverence* and understood that her prayer life had in fact been flagging for some time. I got up there expecting *diligence* or *discipline* or some such thing that I would at least know what to do with.

What I got was *humility*.

I needed to learn humility, they said. Me—who spent half my time reminding everyone how small and frail and fragile I was. Me—who, at nineteen had the habit of crying into my breakfast as I contemplated all the ways in which I had failed myself, God, and the whole wide world. Here I was, the proudest self-loather of the lot, and I was supposed to learn to be humble?

Hot damn, I thought—clearly they had me all wrong.

I didn't get it. For the longest time I didn't get it. In my waking and my sleeping I didn't get it. I thought they gave me that word because I was too spunky or too proud as a vocal and articulate young woman. I imagined they were trying to teach me I was not demure enough, and frankly, it kind of pissed me off.

Who were they to tell me to be humble? Did I not tear myself down often enough to prove how decent and fundamentally innocent I was? Had I not earned my self-loather stripes? Did I not profess my guilt into their ears often enough to inoculate myself against the charge of egotism? I was defensive, fragile, and aggrieved.

It took me years to figure it out. Even now, I sometimes forget. See, even a person who professes their smallness all day long and blathers for everyone to hear about the vast extent of their inadequacy is still fundamentally obsessed with *themself*. Even a person who loudly proclaims their own weakness can still be guilty of imagining they are the center of the universe. Even a card-carrying member of the pity-party lives in a world in which their own needs, their own hopes, and their own failures are paramount, rising above the hopes, needs, desperations, and failures of others.

To be humble without succumbing to the temptation to belittle oneself; to be small without assuming you are insignificant; to be flawed without assuming you are without worth. Those are some of the challenges that come with a practice of authentic humility. It involves giving a true and unvarnished assessment of oneself to oneself and not shying away from it in favor of a more dramatic, polarizing, and self-obsessed answer that burdens other people with the emotional labor of having to forgive you all the freaking time.

Humility is the work of knowing who you are, no more and no less. It means being converted over and over again by that truth into a more gracious and relationally connected version of oneself.

The meditations I learned from the Nashville Dominican sisters finally convinced me, more or less, that I am neither a paragon of innocent virtue nor a wretched little wannabe, hurling my flawed apologies at the great monolith of my failure. Life would be so much more dramatic if either one of those things was true. It would be so much easier to just go about my day being awesome, justified, and right all the time.

It would probably also be reasonably easy to dance back from the edge of my own responsibility by appealing to my inherent inadequacy in the face of, you know, everything. Either way, at least it would be clear.

Since neither of these self-obsessed answers is an actual option, there is a kind of existential reckoning to which I am called daily. This is what the sisters were calling me to when they asked me to meditate on humility. In the classical philosophical form, they wanted me to "know thyself." Then they wanted me to get over myself.

I make no claim that I am adequately engaging in this existential reckoning in my life today. I make no claim that I effectively de-center my own assumptions and neuroses daily through authentic self-assessment and relational accountability. Usually I am just trying not to screw up too badly while paying attention to something—anything—that is not myself. On your average Thursday afternoon, that is about as good as I get on the existential reckoning front.

And yet, that practice of coming to terms with both the failure and the fullness of my own nature is a central task of my spiritual life, given to me by the Catholic tradition I have long since left behind. Daily existential reckoning is an essential component of my moral growth and an important underpinning of any efforts I make toward reconciliation and justice-building in the world.

To my sorrow, I also find that this kind of daily existential reckoning, this practice of encountering the unvarnished self, is not something my adopted religious tradition is often fully equipped to support. Existential reckoning is not in the wheelhouse of the liberal Protestant tradition. We don't really do that anymore. It was, I suppose, too much of a bummer.

Saying the "F" Word

A colleague in ministry, Sean Parker Dennison, has noted that we religious liberals will go to great lengths to avoid either acknowledging or being changed by our own experiences of failure.

As we've seen in previous chapters, this avoidance is historically linked to our high theological anthropology and the old idea that, through proper cultivation and highfalutin self-culture, each soul could be a likened unto God's own self.

Therefore failure, in the plodding course of human existence, translates through liberal Protestant history as an absence of proper cultivation. If you fail, the Protestant tradition teaches, you haven't tried hard enough. Failure is evidence that you are not yet equipped to fully reveal the image of God's face in the course of your own life.

In the liberal Protestant tradition, failure is connected to a false ideal of human perfectibility so powerful it has become an idol, and Denison says that this theological system that measures everyone and everything against perfection has preconditioned us to fear failure so profoundly that we create missions and purposes for the church that are just small enough to succeed at.

> You see, as long as we fear failure—as long as we use up vast amounts of energy trying to be perfect, absolutely and adamantly competent, we are not going to have the energy to be or become the relevant, responsive, passionate, and growing movement . . . we yearn to be. As long as we are frozen in our tracks by the fear that we might fail or more accurately, that others might find out we fail, we are stuck thinking small, making only the safest of plans that we already know will succeed. But I am here to tell you: You might as well go ahead and plan to fail, because you're going to do it anyway. You already are.[51]

This system that professes perfectibility and meets failure with self-protective retreat is more than a little familiar to me. It's pretty much the exact same pendulum swing of self-regard I was trying to interrupt when the Dominican sisters told me to get over myself already.

When gripped jointly by our theology of perfectibility and our overwhelming fear of failure, we can think of nothing but ourselves.

In such a state, we relate to other people, including those we have harmed, not as autonomous individuals with something to share, but as potential vehicles for forgiveness. We reach out with our apologies not because we have already encountered ourselves and been converted to a new way of being, but because somewhere in our hearts we are expecting the one we have harmed to ease our own burdens by offering us ready absolution. We want something in exchange for our apology.

Scholar David Lambert has studied the biblical basis and cultural evolution of repentance in the Jewish tradition. During the 2016 presidential election, he wrote about the tendency among disgraced American political figures to engage in the theater of public apology while continuing to place the emphasis on themselves—the offenders—rather than the ones whom they have repeatedly and egregiously victimized. "One of the biggest problems with repentance," he says, "is that it leaves power in the hands of the victimizer, rather than the victim." He continues,

> The offenders—their feelings, their thoughts, their actions—remain center stage. They control the narrative. When will they choose to apologize? How do they feel about what they've done? In what ways will it transform them for the better? Focusing on repentance can end up enabling a continuation of the very privilege that is often the basis of the most heinous of crimes.[52]

The alternative, of course, is to move the center of attention and action from the oppressors themselves and onto the outcry of those who have been wounded. The feelings of the oppressor are less important than the moral witness of the oppressed. When we commit to re-centering the emphasis in this way, rather than being objects of other people's projections, oppressed people become the subjects of their own stories.

Absolution vs. Atonement

The existential reckoning the Dominican sisters invited me into was related to a fundamental confusion between atonement and absolution. By confessing near and far the greatness of my inadequacy and thereby continuing to hopelessly focus on myself, I was tacitly asking the sisters, my fellow students, and indeed the whole world around me to absolve me for these apparent sins. I was asking them to make me better. I was taking up their time with my own demand for absolution.

However, I was not called to pursue absolution centered on my own internal state of anxiety and external search for validation. Rather, to assume a humble state of atonement in which I was asked to do my own work.

Authentic absolutions imply a willingness not just to be forgiven, but to make amends and to be changed so completely that our actions and reactions can bring us into right relationship with the world and those we share it with.

We do not have the right to request or demand absolution from those we have wounded. For the theists among us, absolution is God's work, not ours. For the universalists among those theists, God's absolution for our sins is almost infinitely available, and our own response in the face of it should be utter and dumbfounded gratitude.

Indeed, whether other people choose to forgive us or not is none of our damn business. Whether or not we are willing to live differently is.

Social justice leader and anti-racist educator Ashley Horan wrote a revised version of the Ten Commandments for white people who wish to engage in "relevant, reparative ministry." In that work, she exhorts white leaders to stop claiming to be allies without first being personally transformed.

She reminds us of the equipping power of spiritual practices to get us ready for the hard work of showing up each time we are called. When she declares, "YOU SHALL NOT KILL," she also exhorts all people of goodwill to "refrain from doing harm, and make amends when we do." She writes,

> We know intent is less important than impact—it matters more that your foot hurts than that I didn't mean to step on it. Our ministry as, and with, white people, then, is to both do less harm in the first place, and when we do, to help our people engage in rituals and processes of confession, atonement, and repair—long before we seek absolution.[53]

Rituals of "confession, atonement, and repair" don't happen after we've begged somebody for forgiveness. They don't happen once we've requested absolution to make our burden lighter. They happen as component parts of a deeper commitment to personal and collective transformation.

These "rituals and processes," Horan implies, are not abstract concepts or ideas. They are not private reflections in sunlit attic rooms, but actual embodied practices that help us come to terms with the harm we have done.

They are part of a public witness that is spoken out loud in the presence of those with whom we share a repeated conversion toward mutuality. Such rituals remind us that no one is in this alone and no one comes through the effort altogether unscathed or wholly innocent.

The rituals and processes of confession and atonement sound an awful lot like foundational work of the church, but the record seems to show that this is work the liberal churches have been more than a little reticent to embrace in recent decades.

When Confession Just Went Away

Not long ago, minister and musician Jason Shelton did a quick study of Unitarian Universalist hymnals to trace the presence of liturgies of confession and repentance over time.

In his survey, he looked at a wide variety of liturgical elements that professed some form of higher aspiration or greater moral purpose for us as individuals or as communities. It was a nice wide net. The results were surprising, if only in their utter clarity. Without looking any further than our denominationally approved books of worship, we can find the approximate time when atonement as a widespread liturgical practice disappeared altogether from the Sunday morning services of most Unitarian Universalists.

The Unitarian liturgical resource *Hymns of the Spirit* was published in 1937. It was the predominant liturgical text in many of our congregations for almost thirty years, and it is full of liturgical elements that draw us into acknowledgment of our shortcomings and compel a motion toward our better selves.

As Shelton points out, some, but not all, of these prayers and liturgies from the 1937 hymnal are overtly theistic in their framing. Included among them is this invitation to humble ourselves before all the wonders, gifts, and "heroisms" of life itself:

> Before the wonders of life we acknowledge our failures to see and to revere; before the sanctities of life we are ashamed of our disrespects and indignities; before the gifts of life we own that we have made choice of lesser goods, and here today seek the gifts of the spirit; before the heroisms of life we would be enlarged to new devotion. Amen.[54]

Shelton prayed this prayer with his congregation just before reminding them that the 1964 Unitarian Universalist hymnal, *Hymns for the Celebration of Life*, contained no such prayers of confession—theistic, atheistic, or otherwise.

Indeed, by 1964 all structurally defined orders of service were gone from our hymnal altogether, inviting congregations into a fully formed practice of liturgical freedom.

Liturgically speaking, by 1964 we were on our own. Congregations and their ministers were fully empowered to choose the content of their services without overt denominational guidance concerning elements of the liturgy. When congregations were freed from liturgical constraint, the first thing that fell away was any kind of liturgical observation of confession or repentance.

It was gone. Between 1937 and 1964, squarely in the middle of the modernist era, Unitarians stopped confessing to anything. We just weren't into that anymore. It wasn't our thing.

I imagine a study of other progressive denominational hymn books would offer up much the same trajectory—if not in the literal erasure of atonement from the liturgy, then at least in a consistent watering down of the practice, sometimes to the point of numb inattention. What progressive Christian congregation has not mumbled their way through that whole part of the liturgy before getting on with communion already?

Right about the same time that the Unitarian Universalists forgot how to atone as a part of the collective spiritual life of our churches, we also seemed to forget that a deep and difficult existential reckoning is important in the work of the church itself. We got so darn busy celebrating life every Sunday that we forgot to authentically examine it.

The great preachers in the liberal tradition over the past fifty years did indeed hold up a mirror to society and decry the idolatries of their age. Some among their number were far braver behind the pulpit than I have ever been. Some asked their congregations to take bold risks out of devotion and commitment. I do not dismiss the work we have done or the impact we have made.

But what we have lacked, for essentially the past half-century, is a gut-level commitment to atonement that would allow us acknowledge that the very systems of oppression those great preachers railed against were birthed in part by the complacency and complicity of the liberal church itself.

We marched with Dr. King in Selma but fizzled in the risk and unsure reward of the poor people's campaign. We decried the atom bomb but continued to serve the military-industrial complex that made it possible. We pounded our fists on the pulpits when we preached against nativism and xenophobia, but have continued, time and again, to center middle-class whiteness almost to the exclusion of all other narratives within our congregations. We fight for the construction of affordable housing, provided it is not located in our own backyards. Some of us even say "Black lives matter," but whisper "all lives matter" to our respectable friends during coffee hour, as if to assure ourselves that we have collectively been on the right side of history all along.

Without robust liturgies and practices that call us to remember, we have forgotten what it feels like to come face to face with the extent of our own shortcomings within the sheltering walls of our own churches. Because of this, we are out of practice with atonement.

The inevitable result is almost too painful to name. Just because the liberal churches have forgotten how to atone does not mean we have ceased to cause harm. And because we do not know how to name the harm we have caused, the mostly white and mostly privileged people among us have outsourced the task of naming our shortcomings to the people whose power is already consistently marginalized.

When a mirror is held up to the mostly white, mostly middle-class, mostly comfortable people in our congregations, it is often held in the hand of a person of color. And since we do not know how to authentically atone, people of privilege in the liberal church respond to this living reflection with defensiveness.

Time and again, when we are asked to see what we would rather not see within ourselves, good liberal believers respond with self-protective, even vicious, declarations of our innocence. Such declarations, while doing nothing at all to deepen or support the spiritual life of the ones defending themselves, do serve as astonishingly effective tools to cause further harm to those who have already been systematically disconnected from community life.

In addition to the harm caused and the hearts broken, what the liberal church tends to miss when we are out of practice with atonement is the sustaining spiritual growth that comes with an authentic encounter with ourselves.

Liturgy, first and foremost, is the work of the people—joined in worship of the highest good and united in pursuit of spiritual honesty and relational depth. As such, liturgy should represent all of the people's spiritual work, including our deep and abiding need to atone.

What if our pastoral prayers were not primarily prayers of praise for an abundant universe or requests for meaning in the midst of great uncertainty? What would it be like if we prayed our atonement out loud instead of mumbling through it or ignoring it altogether? What if we refreshed the words our liberal religious tradition has been avoiding or rushing past for fifty years? Could your congregation or its minister pray out loud, for all to hear, words usually spoken in the silent sanctuary of our own hearts?

In an appendix at the end of this book, see a sample prayer of atonement and some ways to think about whether and how we might add this type of element to our worship services, or use them in other settings.

Metanoia: Every Moment a Prayer

Atonement is difficult, risky work. It can't be done without trust, and it is best practiced in the context of authentic relationships across the boundaries that divide us. It asks us to give life, and breath, and form to our ideals. And let's face it—that kind of thing is always messy.

Yet, in my own life, when I have encountered actual transformation through meaningful atonement, I have never been left bereft of meaning. When I have come face to face with the limitations of my character and the harmfulness of my own choices, I have never been utterly alone.

When the sisters asked me to meditate day and night, night and day on the elusive character of my own humility, they gave me a gift that has gotten me through a hundred dark nights—a spiritual practice that sees me through ministry, motherhood, and the thousand large and small indignities of my life.

Atonement that shifts the focus from oneself and onto the ones with whom we share the journey can be soul food. And the faithful relationships that emerge when we are reconverted toward the will to mutuality can make our activist idealism decidedly more sustainable in the long haul.

If James Luther Adams called the church to thrive and grow through a kind of collective conversion experience, so too are we individually called to a sustained personal spiritual experience of conversion—a process that the great reformer Martin Luther would call metanoia.

Metanoia is derived from an ancient Greek term that originally translated as something like "change of mind" or "alteration of character." In the Christian tradition it is usually communicated as something more like a change of heart, and the early Latin Church fathers often used it to apply to acts of penance or penitence.

Martin Luther believed that all of life should be a consistent and always refreshed practice of metanoia. He taught that we should continually experience a change of heart. We should always be busy being reformed.

This is perhaps an easy opinion for religious progressives to dismiss. Especially if, like Martin Luther, one's understanding of penance is all wrapped up in self-flagellation, hair shirts, and the odd practice of kneeling on stone floors long enough to bleed. Martin Luther had some issues.

But a more expansive understanding of metanoia—one that holds that all of life should be an opportunity for renewal—just might be a form of good news religious liberals are more than ready to preach.

If we live in a constant state of metanoia, we are always receptive because we are always ready to be reborn. We are always willing to learn something new, always willing to hear a story that rests outside of our own realm of experience. Because of this, when we are in a state of metanoia we do not have to waste our energy defending who we are or who we have been, since the constant conversion of our spirit continually invites us to be and become something bolder and more decent than we have been before.

As I write this, we are approaching the highest of high holy days on the Jewish calendar—Yom Kippur, the day of atonement. During this time, believers are called to meaningfully atone for all the harm that they have done and then go a step or two beyond that simple act of acknowledgment—to do something to make it right, to repair what is broken (when possible), and to begin again with a different heart.

In this season, we remember that atonement can be the very beginning of a new kind of freedom—freedom from guilt and shame, replaced by honest reckoning and active commitment.

Rabbi Lawrence Kushner once wrote that in the season of atonement, we should take the evil in ourselves—the parched and burned landscape of our souls—and sweeten it, as if with honey. We should take our broken dreams, our vicious memories, our sins both great and small and bless them for the chance they give us to begin again.

Instead of turning our backs on our wrongdoing, we are called to look directly at it and find the new life that waits, right there, within our dust and ashes.

Kushner says that, at the time of atonement, "We go down into ourselves with a flashlight, looking for the evil we have intended or done—not to excise it as if it were some alien growth, but rather to discover the holy spark within it."[55]

In this way, discovering the holy spark within our own wrongdoing is the whole point of atonement. Not beating ourselves over the head, not self-pity, not a selfish demand for absolution, but the freedom to take our sackcloth and ashes, our shame and guilt and long-ignored suffering, and turn them into a transformed life.

But how do we do this when the liturgies of atonement have all been erased, watered down, or glossed over? How do we go down deep into our souls with a flashlight and find whatever may rest there when we are so darn busy performing our respectability for each other?

How do we submit to the vulnerability required for honest atonement when we are so used to being in control, and how can we trust the liberal church to be a place that will hold that vulnerability with grace and humility?

As with everything else, we must practice it.

There are practices that bring us ever closer to the state of constant metanoia envisioned by the brave ones who went before us. While Martin Luther's hair shirts admittedly go several steps too far for me, I personally (and somewhat bashfully, truth be told) still practice the same invitation to metanoia that I first learned when I was a little girl.

I have been a Unitarian Universalist minister for almost fifteen years. It's obvious that we are not the most doctrinally orthodox people out there. Given that, you may be surprised to know that I pray the traditional formulation of the Orthodox Christian Jesus Prayer over and over every day.

I have done this for most of my life, since long before I found a home in liberal religion. I do so even now because the words are written on my heart in a way that cannot be transferred to any other script.

The theology of the Jesus Prayer would be enough to leave most of the people I serve blanching in anxiety. I have always been a little closeted about the whole thing. But I learned this prayer when I was too young to care if I believed in it or not. I only knew that it helped me. That was, and still is, just about enough for me.

In the Orthodox Church, the Jesus Prayer functions much like the single-word meditation we were given at the Dominican motherhouse. It runs as a kind of subterranean chorus beneath the stuff of life itself. "Lord Jesus Christ, Son of God," it goes, "Have mercy on me, a sinner."

I do not ascribe lordship to God, nor affirm the patriarchal formulation of God's power that it certainly implies. My Christology is low enough to call into question the Son-ship of Jesus altogether, so the second clause is theologically more than a little bit dicey too.

But it's the latter half that keeps me coming back. "Have mercy on me," it pleads. "Have mercy on me, a sinner."

Lord Jesus Christ, Son of God, have mercy on me, a sinner.

I pray those words at least a dozen times a day. Sometimes that whispered prayer is an act of atonement. It is almost never a request for absolution. It's a blessing muttered in the deeper places of my being when I need to acknowledge my dependence on something greater than myself, my commitment to becoming a better version of myself, and my devotion to a life that is sometimes too beautiful to even grasp.

It is a prayer for mercy, because my heart sometimes can't handle either the worry or the glory of life without knowing I am held in abiding relationship to every merciful thing in this fragile world.

When I almost run my car into a passing soccer mom, "Lord Jesus Christ, son of God, have mercy on me, a sinner."

When my four-year-old son inexplicably sniffs my cheek and tells me, "Mommy, you smell like loveliness," "Lord Jesus Christ, son of God, have mercy on me, a sinner."

When I must buck up and go into the meeting and say a hard thing that nobody really wants to hear, "Lord Jesus Christ, son of God, have mercy on me, a sinner."

When the weight in front of me is literally too heavy to lift, and then again after I have lifted it; when my friend is in tears, and when my friend is renewed; when my sermon is crappy, and when grace intervened to help someone find truth in it anyway; when the laundry pile is up to my hips, and I wonder if we'll ever get to sleep tonight, "Lord Jesus Christ, Son of God, have mercy on me, a sinner."

For though I do not believe in the Lordship of God or the literal son-ship of Jesus, though I don't believe in a whole lot of things—that does not mean I am not in need of mercy. That does not mean I am not a sinner. That does not mean I do not stand every day, in a thousand ways, in need of the grace that comes from some force that is greater than me and that includes all of you, especially the people to whom I am most acutely accountable.

The force that is big enough to grant mercy is a force that somehow contains every soul who is hurting and every person I have failed and every leaf that is turning—everything I have ever loved—and I ask for mercy from that interconnected network a dozen times a day, trying to live at least one moment at a time into a state of metanoia that can remake me over and over again.

Longtime clergy leader Rob Eller-Isaacs makes a case that there is much to be learned from the liturgies and practices handed down to us from generations before. The spiritual practice of atonement that sees me through isn't one I created for myself. In fact, it is one that I am sometimes too abashed to share in the life of the liberal church I serve.

And yet, that spiritual practice may be the greatest gift the church has ever given me. Eller-Isaacs preaches and teaches about the necessity of rigorous spiritual practices for religious liberals. More than once, as I have yammered in front of him about my various anxieties, he has looked me squarely in the eye and inquired about the state of my own spiritual practice. Grounded in the utter necessity of these deep practices, Eller-Isaacs recently wrote of what he believes to be the purpose of the church and its ministers:

> I believe the church is in the world to engender the unmediated experience of the Holy in the real lives of real people, our people. . . . I believe that the primary duty of a minister of religion is to design and produce trustworthy rituals that help us to be more loving, more effective human beings.[56]

If progressive religion exists so that real, flawed, weary, and sometimes broken people can encounter the Holy without priestly mediation or doctrinal rigidity, then the liberal church and its ministers must find a way to craft practices and liturgies that invite us into such encounters. Perhaps the liberal church should also be a place where each of us is unashamed of the spiritual practices and touchstones we bring with us into its doors—practices gleaned from lifetimes and generations that came before.

Surely the practices and liturgies of atonement and lament that will see the liberal church through the coming decades will not be carbon copies of the liturgies of a former age. Surely they must be more than the stultifying force of ancient habits—for the minute they become so deeply ingrained in the culture of congregational life as to become routine or hollow, they will again need to be reimagined. Liturgies are like that.

Like people, they are always being reborn.

Eight

Liturgies of Lament

I imagine that one of the reasons people cling to their hates
so stubbornly is because they sense, once hate is gone, that
they will be forced to deal with pain.

—James Baldwin[57]

I had the good fortune of being married at the first Unitarian Church
of Chicago shortly after I was ordained. This means that, through the
course of two simple liturgies in less than a year, I went from being
"Nancy McDonald," to "Rev. Nancy McDonald Ladd." It took me a
while to remember my own name.

Change was afoot in my life. Everything was beginning. Things
were bubbling. Hope was thick like a fog all around us. Most of life
was still waiting to be lived.

Like brides often are, on the day of my wedding I was pinging
with anxiety. It felt to me that being nervous was a culturally man-
dated thing to do on one's wedding day. And I was.

The thing is, though, I wasn't nervous about getting married.
That felt like the natural and altogether awesome next step for the life
I already shared with the person I loved. I also wasn't nervous about
the service itself, the people who were coming to witness it, the food
being served, or the flowers on the altar.

Rather, my anxiety came entirely from playing the weirdly gussied-up role of the bride. I kept adjusting my shoes and
wondering if I looked even a little bit like myself. I felt like a

costumed character in a drama with a grandly choreographed happy ending.

My anxiety stemmed from the fact that I didn't really want to be a bride as such. What I wanted to be was married, to that person, who had himself refused the fancy dress shoes that came with his rented tux.

I wanted to be a real-life person, surrounded by the people I loved, finished with the pomp and circumstance, well and truly started with the life that we were committed to lead together.

I was comforted in my fretting by all the usual things—my mom hovering over me like a member of the heavenly host with a portable hand-held steamer, my sister's marvelously inappropriate whispered commentary. By the fact that the minister was my very best friend and had created an authentic and meaningful liturgy that went way beyond mushy anecdotes and promises of perfection.

All these things were a balm to my soul in a perfectly normal sort of way. But because I am a little odd, and because I was nervous enough to spend a fair bit of time peering around at my surroundings, I was also profoundly comforted by the architecture of the church's sanctuary itself, a sanctuary built for sustaining authentic liturgies.

The night before the wedding, as we were milling about in the way that nervous people do before the serious proceedings begin, someone in our wedding party looked up and noticed the carvings chiseled into the stone surfaces of the great gothic chancel of that church. To one side of the pulpit, in a place only the preacher might see, there stands the combined image of a small cradle and the disembodied head of a chubby baby floating rather disconcertingly above it.

This baby head—artfully wrought, though rather creepy—looks down Sunday after Sunday, year after year at the pageantry of the proceedings below, likely unnoticed by almost all who gather there.

I find this symbol of birth and new life fascinating enough in and of itself, but even more theologically interesting considering the carving that faces it on the opposite side of the chancel there at First

Unitarian Church in Chicago. Indeed, the effect would not be at all complete were it not for the other side of the chancel.

There, exactly mirroring the creepy baby head and the weirdly floating crib, stands an equally creepy image of a coffin and a skull. Like the baby head and crib, these also hover over the Sunday morning proceedings. They do so, however, in the particularly menacing but bad-ass way that only a leering skull and slim-lined coffin possibly could.

A cradle and a grave, an infant and a skull, carved there in the chancel for every preacher who enters that pulpit to see.

We pondered our vows in that chancel, standing both literally and metaphorically between the cradle and the grave. My wedding processional marched me directly beneath them, such that I had one last blessed glance over my shoulder at the deeper things, and the liminal spaces, before I headed up that aisle to meet the tears and wonder and all-around loveliness that did ultimately come along with being a bride.

Surely the chief designer of that space, the great liberal liturgist Von Ogden Vogt, knew exactly what he was doing when he commissioned that design. Surely, he knew that souls across the ages would need to be reminded that they gathered each Sunday morning in both celebration and in sorrow.

One of the most formative influences in the history of progressive liturgy, Vogt was among the first in my tradition to use the phrase "celebration of life" to refer to a service of worship. To him, worship was a dance between polarities—the inner experience and the outer world, the emotional and the intellectual, even the utopian vision of a world made whole and the actual lived experience of a world in pieces.

In his writing, Vogt was captured by the liberal optimism of his day while remaining cognizant of the essential task of liturgy to make room for genuine lament. In 1927, he quoted his friend and co-religionist Guy Allen Tawney, saying, "Worship is like a breathing spell in a long and arduous foot race, or the hour of roll call in a prolonged and hard-fought battle."[58]

Like Von Ogden Vogt, we come into our places of worship both to celebrate the grace that surrounds us and to take solace in the strength beyond our naming. We also come yearning to name what is unravelling in the world and to lament the persistent reality of our broken hearts. We come into our sanctuaries because we are footsore from the long and arduous race, and we come because we crave hope for the journey ahead.

Yet too often, guided by our progressive view of history, our faithfulness in the goodness of humankind, and our long-distance relationship to acts of atonement, we in the liberal church have eagerly taken up the task of delivering up Vogt's "celebration of life," while turning our eyes and hearts away from the polarities that also fueled his vision.

To him, worship consisted not just of a proclamation of good news or the bold sharing of a liberal vision—but a careful attention to all aspects of the human experience, including humble acceptance of the many ways we have collectively fallen short.

I have been in more than one role in the chancel of First Unitarian Church in Chicago. I was a bride there once and have presided there as a minister quite a few times. Therefore, I have had the opportunity to reflect on that architecture while wearing at least two distinctly different hats.

As a bride, I broadly pondered the space between beginnings and endings while wearing my very best clothes, taking comfort in the larger story of which I was but one small part. As a preacher, I am keenly aware that the bright beginnings symbolized by the chubby stone cheeks of the creepy baby only exist in relationship to the haunted hollow eyes of the leering skull on the other side, and that every word I speak in the chancel must have relevance to the very specific triumphs and looming losses of the people I serve.

When thoughtfully conceived, our worship and our spiritual practices invite us not just into a gussied-up version of our own story, but also into the liminal space between bright beginnings and irretrievable loss. Everything we do stands somewhere along the journey from the dawn to the dusk, and our liturgies must reflect both the fullness of our gratitude and the depths of our sorrow.

From a pastoral perspective, liturgies that engage with lament, loss, and suffering invite the encounter with the holy that Rob Eller-Isaacs names as the primary purpose of the church in the world—an encounter that changes us and gives us a fighting chance of being renewed by our living rather than just enduring it.

Eventually, if we are not engaging with words and liturgies of lament, the reality of the world crashes up against the celebration of life taking place in liberal churches every Sunday morning. The disconnection can be all too jarring, causing significant pain.

It is not enough to celebrate the glory of life or the wonder of nature when four hurricanes are bearing down on Cuba. It is not enough to gather together in utmost gratitude for the glories of creation when people are dying at the hands of their oppressors. A church whose liturgy knows only the celebration of human triumph or the meek acknowledgment of human loss sacrifices both its relevance and its transformative power.

Echoing the sentiments of James Luther Adams, Rev. Dr. William Wallace Fenn, onetime dean of Harvard Divinity School, captured this inadequacy of unending good news when he wrote in 1913,

> Turning now to the criticism of Liberalism from within, to which its own creative principle gives rise, we must seriously raise the question whether it can bear the weight of the tragedies of human experience. Does not its amiable faith in inherent goodness but appear ghastly mockery when confronted by the facts of life? . . . We would not have Modern Liberalism return to a belief in the devil—that is too easy a solution to the problem—but it must deal more justly with the crushing tragedies of life, with evil and sin, if it is to command the respect of candid and thoughtful men. The saviors of the world have always been and always will be men of sorrow and acquainted with grief.[59]

Indeed, the saviors of the world have been people of every age, gender expression, story, and creed, whose lives of courage demanded that they become well and thoroughly "acquainted with grief."

There are no great ones who did not weep. There are no heroines who did not suffer, and there are no prophets who were not, sooner or later, persecuted for the risky truth that they spoke.

For Those Who Could Not Look Away

In 1998, I took a trip to El Salvador with friends and fellow radicals aligned with the Catholic Worker movement. This was in the wake of the Salvadoran Civil War, when violence raged across the countryside from 1980 to 1992. During that time more than 75,000 civilians in El Salvador died at the hands of government forces.

The sources of the conflict are as old as colonialism itself, dating back to the sixteenth century, when the Spanish effectively turned the whole country into a massive plantation operation and its proud indigenous peoples into serfs in service to a shockingly small minority of wealthy landholders of European ancestry.

This plantation state persisted well into the twentieth century until resistance groups joined together in armed response. Whole villages suspected of complicity with the resistance were brutalized in the most horrific forms imaginable.

My progressive social-justice-oriented friends and I went to El Salvador five years after the end of the war to follow gently in the footsteps of these martyrs. We went to pay homage to those who refused to shield their eyes or their hearts from the reality of economic oppression and wholesale slaughter, and to mourn those who could not have looked away even if they tried.

We walked along shaded lanes near the Honduran border, where white butterflies once flitted gracefully past gutters filled with corpses. We prayed in the places where praying was once an act of profoundly dangerous resistance.

It was not a service trip. It was a pilgrimage wrapped up in worship, and the worship we encountered at every corner was inextricably interwoven with the people's abiding and almost unimaginable grief.

One sunlit afternoon we visited the University of Central America (UCA) in San Salvador, and we sat in sun-dappled silence while contemplating the Salvadoran Stations of the Cross.

These images, in black lines on white background, do not show Jesus carrying his burden or hanging on his cross. They don't show the traditional passion narrative at all, a story of suffering familiar enough to be often overlooked in the dust-covered niches of a thousand churches.

Instead, the Stations of the Cross at the UCA show the beaten and barbed-wired bodies of El Salvador's dead. The twisted backs of the tortured. The pierced skin of the resistance fighters. The wailing eyes of mothers. The ones who were struck down because they refused to be silent.

The Stations of the Cross in that place are not theological reminders of someone else's suffering. For the people who worship there, they are tangible evidence of the devastation they have known. They are images of Good Friday that acknowledge the vast distances yet to cross before we ever get to Easter morning.

Looking at those images as the pure sunlight of a summer day filled the sanctuary was almost more than I could bear—and all I did was sit there in perfect safety and pray. All I did was walk the shady lanes long after the blood had all been cleared away. All I did was bear witness to the aftermath of the destruction. The idea of coming home to my own sunlit sanctuary to celebrate life on Sunday morning, earnest and unknowing, all full of profound declarations of bright beginnings, dug a hole out under my heart.

There was no room in El Salvador for any variety of hope that didn't acknowledge despair. It was not possible, really, to look away. The hope that could be built from those ashes was a hope that could not even for a moment deny the immensity of the loss.

In this way, the Stations of the Cross we beheld with muffled chokes and barely concealed sobs weren't morbid. They certainly weren't cynical, and they also weren't evidence of some eventual triumph that would ultimately be gained through the suffering of the people.

The images on those walls were just true. They were honest and unflinching witness to the pain the people of El Salvador and the worshippers in that congregation had borne, the pain that people bore even still, the pain that even comfortable people in times of relative peace should not be entirely allowed to ignore.

The images served as a testimony to a truth more horrible than I had previously imagined, and a survival more miraculous than I can even now conceive. They were terrifying, never beautiful, always real.

The church in which those images hang is a place to go to meet the holy, to feel the pain and honor the struggle, to experience the change of heart that is necessary to build a world in which such horrors cannot happen again. It is a place of conversion, and that conversion from death and toward life is itself a source of hope.

Such liturgies of lament, struck through with the evidence of terror and unflinching honesty, are present in many of the worship traditions of oppressed peoples. These liturgies of lament are not intended to make people feel comfortable. They are designed to communicate the truth.

Something Ghastly, Something True

Not long ago, I attended an interfaith rally in the wake of violence that came to Charlottesville, Virginia, in the summer of 2017, when racist extremists burst into town with their hatred and their tiki torches and their instruments of death.

I needed to be with my coreligionists that day. I needed to be with my friends. Clergy from every faith tradition stood together to bear witness to the power of love and the depth of our responsibility to each other. We wept and hugged and confessed and proclaimed, and near the end of the service, a chorus of mostly Black labor leaders and unionists rose up to sing the gripping refrain of the Black National Anthem.

"Lift every voice and sing," proclaim the lyrics of James Weldon Johnson, "till earth and heaven ring, ring with the harmonies of liberty."

In the Black church tradition, the people stand when the anthem starts. They raise their hands, ball their fists, and grasp their neighbors on the arm while singing the words that are uniquely endowed to Black Americans through their history of oppression and courageous resistance. The lyrics carry on fearlessly and without flinching:

We have come over a way that with tears has been watered,
We have come, treading our path through the blood of the
    slaughtered;
Out from the gloomy past, till now we stand at last
Where the white gleam of our bright star is cast.[60]

We stood together after the death and the terror of Charlottesville, led by African-American voices in this proclamation of pain and triumph. And after all the words and all the talking and all the statements of heartfelt intent, this liturgical moment from a tradition that is not my own brought me to tears.

Here, truly, was a liturgy of lament. Here, truly, was an authentic encounter with the broken-open heart of the holy. Here, truly, was church being church.

Afterward, making my way to the door, I overheard a white woman leaning in to her friend to discuss how moving the service had been. What a lovely service, she said. But that song! That song with all the blood and the slaughtering. That song, she said—so ghastly.

And do you know what I did? Me, who had been pondering these things in my heart since seminary? Do you know what I did? I just walked away. Because I thought I might fall over, because of my privilege and my caution and the fact that I did not, strictly speaking, have to engage—I walked away, never mentioning that the song is ghastly because history is ghastly, that the song is triumphant because history is triumphant, that the people declare words of slaughter and blood and power because such words, in the context of history, are the only words that are true.

I walked away and did not say out loud that people of color are under no obligation to tone it down so that white people can feel more comfortable and less inconvenienced by the presence of a gripping, ghastly truth like white supremacy. I walked away, damn it all—and one of the reasons we need practices of atonement is because that moment was neither the first nor the last time I declined to tell the truth; have mercy on me.

One of the reasons we need liturgies of lament is because some among us persist in believing that truth-telling is a form of ghastly unpleasantness, and some of us cannot continue to worship in a community that isn't equipped to attend to the truth of our lives, even when that truth is profoundly and unassailably painful.

Attending to Each Other's Pain

Never forget, a teacher of mine once said, that every Sunday morning when you rise to preach, someone in that congregation has just suffered the broken heart that they will spend a lifetime trying to mend. Never forget that someone in that congregation has just found a way through some great desolation. Never forget that someone in that congregation is here for the first time, wondering if this will be yet another place where they won't be noticed, won't be seen, won't be cared for. And somewhere in that congregation there is someone grappling with a choice that will remake their life.

Every Sunday morning, the people are arrayed in the sanctuaries of the liberal churches. Their stories, heartbreaks, hurts, and triumphs are safely contained, for the length of the prelude at least, by the propriety and convention that wrap themselves around the act of worship.

There they are, with their complex stories and their broken hearts and their limitations and their sins. There they are, all of them. Every Sunday morning. There they are. Waiting together for an honest word.

Preaching professors have taught that if you throw out the entire rule book of the craft of homiletics, if you just go ahead and toss away every text ever written on how to be a more effective preacher and cleave only to one single thing, it should be the imperative to preach good news.

Always preach good news. That, some say, is the primary responsibility of the preacher. Never leave them hopeless.

In my seminary classes, I learned a particular homiletic device that we called the "oops–whee" sermon. This is just one strategy among many. You don't want to do an oops–whee every Sunday, of course—that would be boring—but its basic structure is fairly easy, so one is tempted to deploy it with some frequency.

To do an oops–whee sermon, you build out about ten minutes or so of a problem. This problem could be a spiritual or a social situation—when it comes to form, it does not really matter. In those ten minutes the preacher should go about explaining the depth of the "oops" in which we are caught and the struggle that is now before us.

Then, in the second act of the sermon, through some artfully constructed turn, structured as to be barely perceptible to the listener, the preacher moves ultimately to the "whee." This, of course, is the arc of hope. If that preacher is very, very good, the final turn of the sermon moves the gathered people toward some individual or collective action. Like I said, easy enough.

I've preached some oops–whees in my day. I'm sure I'll do them again. I'll worry my listeners to no end at the beginning, but bring it nicely back to resolution by the end. I'll have people hoping beyond hope before the last song is sung. Like a good minister must, I'll find the good news and I will share it.

But I increasingly find that the craft of preaching isn't about finding our way to an unmitigated "whee" by the time the postlude plays. Some Sundays we do not need to leave the sanctuary dancing. Some Sundays we need to walk out of the sanctuary having experienced a deeper connection to a deeper truth than we could have named when we walked in.

That deeper connection can be troubling, unsettling, beautiful, darkly humorous, and heart-rending. It can move us without assuring us that everything will be okay in the end. Good news, I have heard it said, doesn't always mean good times.

Echoing a reality often expressed by central American liberation theologians, Duke religious studies Professor Joseph R. Winters has written that Black literary and aesthetic tradition holds within itself the capacity to gesture "toward a different kind of hope." This tradition tells the truth of history as experienced by marginalized people and offers a way forward toward the future that is not tainted by narratives of middle-class comfort and respectability.

This different kind of hope, Winters says, is distinct in form from the hope most often proclaimed in the more comfortable middle-class white-dominated cultural spaces. It is a hope that contains a healthy dash of melancholy and a barely contained humor about to burst out of the respectability that surrounds it. It's a hope that exists alongside the people's willingness to engage the world without looking away or slipping into a posture of self-defense.

This hope, born from within the traditions of marginalized peoples, feels bold or risky in mostly white churches and in mostly white cultural spaces precisely because it is authentic. And because it is authentic, it feels vulnerable. As Winters writes,

> This melancholic hope, in opposition to triumphant, over-confident narratives, tropes, and images, suggests that a better, less pernicious world depends partly on our heightened capacity to remember, contemplate, and be unsettled by race-inflected violence and suffering.[61]

A better world depends on our ability to intentionally encounter suffering without seeking to minimize or distract from the particular intensity of the authentic narrative being shared.

In an authentic liturgy of lament, pain is neither fetishized nor minimized. It isn't handed over freely from marginalized communities for interpretation through the perceptions, words, and experiences of a dominant culture. It isn't gazed upon from a safe distance or engaged with as a problem that those who are not experiencing can solve on behalf of the burdened or the broken or the oppressed.

In my ministry, I have had too many occasions to create and officiate liturgies of lament. More than I care to remember, in fact. From one shooting after another to the sudden and shattering loss of young life in my own congregation, I've stood in those fires. I don't claim to have a path worked out that results in meaningful liturgies of lament for the pain of all the people, but I have ideas of what works and doesn't work—some of them born of hard experience. Some of these ideas are included in an appendix at the end of this book. It doesn't provide answers, just one pastor's efforts, one liturgist's trials and errors.

Even if our liturgies and efforts are imperfect vessels for the immensity of our people's grief, attending to the real pain present in our communities is nothing short of sacred work, and ignoring it—or glancing away—can be a form of erasure for those of us whose relationship to injustice is anything but abstract.

As an African-American man with a broken heart, freelance writer Shane Paul Neil describes his own experience during and after the racist violence in Charlottesville, Virginia. Wondering if his safety and well-being mattered in his own country, he reflects on what it feels like to move in mostly white spaces immediately after the events in question. He speaks of the offensiveness of his own pain, and the constant burden of not being acknowledged in the white-centered spaces of his own life:

> I'm on my way to a job where I am the only Black person in my office. I work with people who either don't know or don't care about Alton Sterling or Philando Castile. They are going to ask me "how are you this morning?" and the simple truth is that I can't be honest. I can't say that I'm scared and angry and that I want to take a mental health day. I can't say that I and people like me subconsciously fear for our lives on a daily basis. I can't say how I am this morning because

it will make them uncomfortable and offended. The offensiveness of my pain is why we have to remind America over and over again that Black Lives Matter: because if you lack empathy for our tears it's likely that you lack respect for our lives.[62]

Indeed, it is the offensiveness of pain, the ghastliness of honest liturgies, and the avoidance inherent in the liberal tradition that prevent us from the authentic encounters that make soul-level change and authentic conversion toward mutuality possible.

We can bid one another "good morning," but only with the expectation that the morning truly has been particularly good. We can greet one another with warmth and attentiveness, as long as what we receive in return fits our expectations of what "good news" feels like on a Sunday morning. We can handle the "oops," but only if we are quickly handed a "whee" to make it all feel a little bit better.

The challenge, of course, is that we cannot love more deeply if our hearts don't break together, and our hearts can't break together if we can't hear each other's stories. Some Sunday mornings, a melancholy hope that does not tip toward triumph may be the only kind of authentic hope there is.

Natalie Fenimore, who, like me, came to Unitarian Universalism from a different tradition, has said that her faith of origin was a "testifying religious tradition, not a confessing tradition." To her, this testimony means that the people share their pain with one another. It means that they speak it out loud. Most importantly, it means that when pain is called into the room, "everybody in that room is called to attend to it."

Attending to each other's pain is holy and difficult work. It's inherently relational. It means that we must listen. Fenimore goes on to say that it's easy enough for a liberal religious tradition that struggles to identify its own liturgy of lament to "steal" from the traditions of other people and other worshipping bodies.

It's easy enough for white people to take the liturgies of others and adapt them to their use. It's a whole different commitment for the liberal congregations to use our worship as an opportunity to behold the perspectives, stories, and conceptual frameworks brought to the table of congregational life by people of color both inside and outside the church. As Fenimore says,

> There are things I've learned in the African-American religious community, things I hear from people in the Hispanic Catholic tradition, things I hear from the Muslim traditions, from indigenous peoples of faith. This knowledge and experience can enrich Unitarian Universalism. When I am invited into Unitarian Universalism, when those from these other traditions are invited in, all that they have to offer must be invited in.[63]

We crave liturgies that heal. We need communal practices that pull us out of our own expressed need for comfort and into a shared will toward mutuality. We are called to experience worship that transforms us so that we can serve meaningfully alongside others. And the only way to build these liturgies is to welcome the pain of our reality into the sanctuary doors instead of using the church to shelter ourselves from it.

What would it look like, and what would it feel like, my colleague Glen Thomas Rideout asks, if the white voices in mostly white choirs could "sing spirituals with a certain authoritative understanding of their own inadequacy and a certain deep willingness to stay in the learning relationship of the song?"

Then, he says, "We will know we've pushed further in the right direction."

What would it look like for a mostly white choir to sing a song of brokenness that isn't externalized, out there, beyond their experience? What would it look like if Sunday morning was just the outward form of a deeply authentic network of relationships across boundaries of difference that had already changed the lives of the worshippers long before the candles were lit and the music played? Some days we touch that feeling in the congregation I serve. Some days we do not. Always we yearn for something that compelling and authentic.

What if worship was just the public expression of the deep relational intimacy that has already busted us wide open with love for one another? What would it feel like if liberal religion acknowledged the broken hearts of its own people such that every sanctuary and every "celebration of life" could also authentically honor the liminal spaces of our own inadequacy and the tightrope we all walk between death and life?

Nine

Fundamentally Estranged, Inextricably Interconnected

Thus, the state of our whole life is estrangement from others and ourselves, because we are estranged from the Ground of our being, because we are estranged from the origin and aim of our life. And we do not know where we have come from, or where we are going. We are separated from the mystery, the depth, and the greatness of our existence. We hear the voice of that depth; but our eyes are closed. We feel that something radical, total, and unconditioned is demanded of us, but we rebel against it, try to escape its urgency, and will not accept its promise.

—Paul Tillich[64]

Back in the heady days of seminary, right before the Twin Towers fell and a year or so before I entered parish ministry, my streak of realism and dash of cynicism were offset by the power and possibility that seemed to stir in the very air around me.

Even I, with my healthy suspicion of liberal optimism well in place, found myself touched by the white fire of the reformer's spirit. Every tempest in every teapot—along with every motion toward perfection—was mine to grasp if only I stayed awake to the moment of opportunity. I was finding my way in my new religious home. And the way stretched out before me in a promising enough fashion. I had a year of seminary left to go. Things were looking up.

Yet amid all that good, solid, soul-stirring progressivism, I did what a great many young people of my generation eventually need to do—I went home. I was broke, of course, as any good graduate student is at some point, and I found myself back in southern Indiana, between school terms, hanging out with my parents, looking for a summer job, and sorting out some of the legacy of what I'd left behind.

I was back in the shadow of the dead utopias. This time, instead of cleaning hotel rooms at the inn or trying to keep ahead of the mountains of dishes that piled up in the rental cottages of the town's profusion of poets-in-residence, I got a gig as a historical interpreter and tour guide. For the first time, I was the one wearing the bonnet and churning the butter.

This time it was me telling stories about the sweeping wave of utopian idealism that tore through the United States in the middle of nineteenth century. This time it was me making sense of our crumbled utopian legacies, and this time I had the chance to place the progressive fervor I learned about as a child in relationship to the progressive fervor that surrounded me in my seminary education.

That summer, I walked around again in the peaceful streets of New Harmony, Indiana. I thought about the failures of perception and the faithfulness to abstractions that characterized the storied history of my own home. I thought about the reformist vision of my new liberal faith while pondering all the ways that the New Moral World fell short in my town.

During all this wandering and all of this pondering, I asked myself what shadows we might all live under two hundred years hence—when the idealistic progressive reforms of my generation had all run their courses and the straight lines we had so fearlessly set out between the world as it is and the world as it should be had all gone crooked in the steady march of time.

In a manner reserved almost exclusively for well-tended white girls with good feminist boyfriends and a social safety net, I also spent my time indulging in a healthy dose of morose existentialist theologizing. I sat about memorizing Macbeth's entire dyspeptic monologue just for the sheer delicious melancholy of its sound on my lips.

"Tomorrow and tomorrow and tomorrow creeps at this petty pace from day to day, to the last syllable of recorded time," I recited to myself while waiting for tourists who mostly did not come, "and all our yesterdays have lighted fools the way to dusty death."

Life, I pondered—along with daring vision and grand ambition and moral purity—really is just a poor player strutting around a stage of our own devising. In the end, dust claims our abstract ideals and all our boldest enterprises blow away to nothingness. All of this brooding was very dramatic indeed. I rather enjoyed it.

As I brooded, I waited for the meaning inherent in the dead utopias of my ancestral home to somehow make itself clear to me. I wallowed in the grand melancholy of it all because I was blessed enough to do so, knowing that such self-indulgent reveries would eventually need to resolve themselves into the stuff of actual life again.

Even during my brooding, I knew that neither paternalistic reformist zeal nor deliciously disengaged cynicism was the answer. The glory of my own melancholy was not a particularly effective way forward. So I went looking around the little town of New Harmony for different ways to begin again. I was looking for something outside of the safety and self-satisfaction of either cynicism or disconnected idealism.

I did not find all the answers, but I did have one more chance to integrate the dead utopias that had gone before with the dying utopia of liberal optimism I was just about to return to in seminary.

Existential Estrangement in a Strange Little Town

When I was a kid growing up around New Harmony in the 1980s, the undisputed town matriarch was a mysterious grand dame named Jane Blaffer Owen. Everybody in the town seemed to work for her in one way or another. Most people called her "Jane" behind her back, but always "Mrs. Owen" to her face.

She rode all around town on a tatted-up old golf cart and resided in a quiet cottage adjacent to the old Rapp mansion. There was a truly lovely tire swing in her side yard, though to this day I am not certain if I was trespassing on the multiple occasions that I dared to swing on it.

Mrs. Owen was not just the owner of that lovely tire swing and the adjacent well-kept cottage. She and her husband, Kenneth Dale Owen, were in fact the owners of about half of the town, including the old Rapp mansion. That is where Mr. Owen was said to live, though I confess that I never once actually saw the man in person.

They were estranged, I understood—living across the street from one another in a quiet standoff since sometime around 1960. The old mansion was kept in immaculate condition, but nobody ever seemed to set foot within it or even on its grounds—not even to catch a glimpse of the massive stone on the lawn that old Father Rapp once claimed bore the footprint of the Angel Gabriel himself.

Because of this fascinating legacy of 150 years of Owens in New Harmony and the slightly spooky undertones of the whole situation, I looked on with curiosity as Jane Owen zipped by me on the sidewalks in her golf cart, leaving a comet-tail of silky scarves and an aura of mystery behind her. I never spoke to her, but her presence was everywhere.

Mrs. Owen, it turns out, had spent several of her formative years studying at Union Theological Seminary in New York with some of the great progressive reformers of the twentieth century. She personally knew James Luther Adams, who was just "Jim" to her. She also studied and learned alongside the famed German theologian Paul Tillich, a character whom locals describe today as "that high-minded foreigner she was always talking about."

Paul Tillich was indeed a high-minded foreigner. He was not from around there. The great man had found his way to Union seminary in the 1930s after being fired from his teaching post when Hitler rose to chancellor and used the first waves of his power to get rid of any academics or public figures who chanced to criticize him in public; Tillich had traveled all around to German universities giving lectures that did just that. When the Nazis clamped down on intellectuals, the wise professor was quick to jump at the chance dangled in front of him by fellow theologian

Reinhold Niebuhr to come shape young American minds in New York City.

The young American minds he shaped included that of Jane Blaffer Owen, whose devotion to both Tillich himself and to his existential theology continued for the rest of her long life.

In fact, Tillich's ashes are interred right there in New Harmony in a massive shade-filled garden that she had built for him, complete with a looming sculpture of the theologian's head. As a one-time maid in the town's fanciest restaurant, one of my great personal mortifications happened when I accidentally stained the carpet in the perfectly decorated "Tillich Room" that overlooked that peaceful garden.

That embarrassment at staining the carpet in the Tillich Room constituted the full extent of my knowledge of this profoundly important twentieth-century theologian until that brooding summer in the middle of seminary when I walked around town looking for answers outside of my own cynicism.

When I did go looking, it turned out there were plenty of alternatives to both utopianism and cynicism right there at my fingertips. I really didn't have to look too far.

Tillich himself had once preached a rousing sermon on Pentecost of 1963 right there in New Harmony. It encapsulated some of the most stirring theological work of his later life and offered a profoundly important corrective to the visionary but disconnected optimism of the Owenite dream.

On that bright Pentecost Sunday morning, in a church under the open sky dedicated to an ecumenical religious ideal he shared with Jane Owen and Jim Adams, Tillich preached a message about the fundamental estrangement inherent in the social structures of the modern age, when people were increasingly disconnected from themselves, from the ground of their being, and—perhaps most importantly—from each other.

There in New Harmony, on the ground of the failed utopia—he called for what he dubbed a whole different kind of new harmony, a return to the connectedness and interdependence in which actual change is possible.

"All our lives we are estranged," he said, "and others are estranged from us." This fundamental estrangement, he said, is nearly universal and to some degree also eternal. It is a pivotal aspect of what it means to be a human being.

It does not hold, however, that the degree of this estrangement we live in is utterly outside of our own hands. We have agency. We can make choices. And while God, the ground of our being, reaches out through grace to bring us back into relationship again, we can also use our significant capacities to reach for a new level of connectedness and interrelationship in our own personal and spiritual lives.

Estrangement is the state of our being, but we do not have to submit to it entirely. "Now what is the estrangement which requires a new reunion, a new harmony?" he asked.

> It is the estrangement of man from his true being in a three-fold way: the estrangement from the ground of being, the estrangement from himself, and the estrangement from all those with whom he lives. All religions, all social action, all healing attempts, and all forms of healing have tried to overcome these estrangements. We have realized in our century, perhaps more than ever before, the estrangement of every person from himself and his true being.[65]

As I read and re-read those words today, I can finally understand what ached in my heart when I first discovered the liberal religious tradition I still love so much. I can begin to grasp the origins of my discomfort with progressive optimism and my generation's dis-ease with the brazen self-assurance of the liberal religious leaders who came before us.

Reading those words, I can finally see that it isn't only the optimism of the liberal tradition that feels hollow and empty to me, nor was it the optimism of the Owenite dream that spelled its downfall and turned my radically conceived hometown into a mostly white haven for privileged poets to be inspired by.

It wasn't just the bold eschatology of a progressivist view of history, pointing always toward the world as it should be, that left me hungry and disaffected with the liberal church—nor was it merely Robert Owen's unflappable faith in the grand possibility of the human endeavor that alienated his followers almost as soon as his experiment had begun.

It wasn't the optimism that killed utopia in my hometown. And it isn't a brightly hopeful progressive vision itself that continually undercuts the power and possibility of liberal religion today. It wasn't (and isn't) even the galling and unexamined arrogance of the progressive dream that posed the most foundational problem.

The problem was, and still is, the estrangement.

Rather than simply being too optimistic, Robert Owen was desperately ensnared in his own triply debilitating estrangement. Estrangement from himself, estrangement from the holy, and estrangement from the community in which he sought to plant his reforms. He lived almost entirely in the world of his own ideals. A force unto himself, his reforms were birthed in the safe and self-assured privacy of his own mind.

Since he spent his days living in relationship primarily with himself and his own vision, Owen was chronically and unremittingly disconnected, and while the Eurocentric white liberal churches grew over the course of the twentieth century to embody a bold reformist vision rather similar to his own, they also adopted a similar and abiding triple estrangement from their own deepest truths, the disquieting call of the holy, and the communities in which they were destined to live and move and have their being.

Earlier in this book, I laid out the corrupting forces that spelled the ultimate demise of the secular utopia in my hometown—forces that are at work in the utopian imagination of liberal religion in America.

Those broadly stated forces of estrangement and disconnection include:

- A profound and sometimes naive faith in the upward trajectory of history, guided by an equally profound and equally naive faith in humanity's capacity to affect that upward trajectory of change.

- This faith in human capacity, while abstractly universalist in character, is mostly circumscribed around a very specific set of people—usually a small circle of uniformly elite, largely male, and overwhelmingly white intellectuals—who personally construct a broadly stated vision that lays claim to their ultimate loyalty.

- A habit of parachuting in from out of town or out of context on projects of benevolent paternalism that are not grounded in authentic relationship to the communities in which such reforms are planted.

- An inability or persistent refusal on the part of the privileged reformers to place themselves within their social location or to acknowledge and atone for the ways in which they have benefited from the oppression of others.

Those corrupting forces contributed to the demise of the various utopian visions that sparked the New Harmony experiment, and those forces contribute to the increasingly tenuous grasp on relevance that liberal religion in America clings to today.

Significantly, those corrupting forces can be traced back to a fundamental estrangement on the part of the progressive reformers themselves. Then, as now, we are estranged from ourselves, from the holy, and from each other. Then, as now, we can use our power and our agency to choose to live differently.

The Self, the Ground of Being, and One Another

Estrangement from the deeper truths of one's own selfhood gives rise to the persistent self-deceptions that have plagued liberal reformers since well before the nineteenth century. As we saw through the history of the New Harmony experiment, virtually no one could equal Robert Owen's unfailing faithfulness in his own capacities. He truly believed that he had hit upon the ultimate answers to life's most vexing questions and could not countenance a version of his own story in which he may, perhaps, have been wrong.

And so his self-deception, combined with his commitment to the continual perpetuation of that self-deception, estranged him from himself. He fooled himself into believing he had it all figured out, and this estrangement made him both ineffective and, at times, pitiable. Having lost four-fifths of his total worth in the failed experiment that was New Harmony, Owen publicly insisted until the end of his life that it had been a grand success.

In the liberal religious tradition, our estrangement from our deepest selves is also connected to the self-deceptions we create and perpetuate. When atonement disappears from our liturgies and lament is papered over in favor of triumphalism, we lose our ability to relate to our own honest stories.

When we adopt a theological anthropology that declares us to be almost infinitely powerful agents of moral change in the world, we proclaim an oversimplified self-identity that robs us of our capacity to listen to the voices of the people with whom we share the struggle. When we conceive of ourselves as made in the image of a God that looks and speaks and acts and chooses according to the standard norms of middle-class white America, we have abandoned the potential depth of our own tradition.

When we in the liberal church are at our worst, we struggle with great ferocity to maintain these self-deceptions. Among the privileged persons who have held power in progressive institutions for generations, our own complicity in the oppression of others has been alchemized into innocence by repeated declarations of our own inherent goodness.

Like Robert Owen, we too have sometimes fooled ourselves into believing that our disconnected reforms have been grand successes, and through our estrangement from ourselves, we have lost touch with beautiful, blessed, and painfully flawed deeper truths.

If an authentic encounter with one's own deeper self can happen in the life of the liberal church, it will be forged through liturgies of lament and authentic acts of atonement. As Rob Eller-Isaacs said, it will happen when we invite "unmediated experience of the Holy in the real lives of real people."

This holiness we are called to encounter may not translate, as in orthodox traditions, to a sentient or separate entity we may know as God. Paul Tillich himself offered an alternative ontology of the divine that held that the holy itself is beyond form. Famously, he held that God is not a being as such, capable of intervening in human affairs, but the ground of all being itself.

Thus the existence of God as a separate entity becomes a pointless debate, since God's self is the essence of being. This, he said, is a distinctly different theology from what he called theological theism. Holiness is born not through faith in some wholly externalized force, but in the divine–human encounter. All the good stuff happens in the fleeting and sacred moments when human beings behold the ground of our own being, the essence from which we arise.

By no means a traditional theological theist, Robert Owen did not believe that a supernatural force could respond to the invocation of human will through direct machinations in the lives of people. He especially did not believe that any such force could or should be mediated by sanctimonious and antiquated structures like religious institutions. Owen believed that we were created entirely through the specific circumstances of our own lives. While those circumstances put us into relationship with the world around us, the dependence of each person upon the greater whole was overshadowed by the power of our own personal vision.

In this way, Owen was estranged from his own socially constructed identity. He only related meaningfully to his own vision. While he often proclaimed that the character of each person is utterly dependent on the inputs they receive, he lived as if he himself was the generative principle through which the most important ideas arose.

For liberal Protestants in America, a relationship to the ground of being reminds us that no one arises individually into the world with a self-contained and fully formed vision. We are called into awareness of our own dependence and the pull of our interconnection with that which moves not only within us, but also among us and beyond us altogether.

If there is a God who calls in the lives of liberal religious people, it is a bold and irksome God, one who moves in demanding ways to shift us from complacency and into deeper courage. It is a God who demands conversion away from the will to power and toward the will to mutuality.

By focusing almost entirely on the power and possibility of each person's individual effort (and sometimes each person's individual innocence), liberal churches have become estranged from this forceful ground of being on which we are utterly dependent. By proclaiming a form of good news that presumes our own capacity to affect an endlessly upward trajectory of history, we have undermined our ability to authentically encounter that which is larger than ourselves.

And the larger context upon which we are dependent has everything to do with the actual people with whom we share the journey. Tillich's third and perhaps most essential form of estrangement, expressed in the dualistic gender language with which he was accustomed, was humankind's "estrangement from those with which he lives."

This form of estrangement—from actual people with actual experiences and actual needs—was perhaps the most striking form of disconnection evidenced in the New Harmony experiment.

For all his reformer's zeal, Robert Owen remained fundamentally separated from people at every level of his new society. Back at the New Lanark Mill, he saw people as test subjects in his own larger scheme of reform. In New Harmony, the people lived in common, but the financial tenuousness of the whole situation meant that he held the deed to the property. While Owen himself never lost faith in the perfection of his own ideals, his perception of the real needs of the people around him was often pitiably off-base.

In 1826, the Duke of Saxe-Weimar, a wealthy Austrian noble, was engaged in a grand tour of the American continent, recording his impressions for his eager readers back home. Since the Owenite experiment had been making headlines all over the world, the Duke made certain to stop over in the Hoosier utopia before moving on to the vastness of the Western states.

After meeting Owen, touring the town and talking with its citizens, the Duke managed to grasp the vast distances between Mr. Owen's perception and the lived experience of the people there. "It grieved me," he said, "to see that Mr. Owen should be so infatuated by the passion for universal improvement as to believe and assert that he is about to reform the whole world, and yet that almost every member of his society with whom I talked acknowledged that he was deceived in his expectations."[66]

Owen landed in New Harmony with his vision already in place, complete and fully formed. He came to share that vision with all who could come to hear it, and he never did consider the necessity of forming or reforming his plans around the actual experiences, self-professed stories, and tangible needs of the people he hoped his reforms would serve.

To him, the people were almost an afterthought. It was the vision that was important. For Robert Owen, it was the idea itself that was salvific. And the salvific idea was always his alone to share.

Like Owen, many of the refined intellectuals on the Boatload of Knowledge were fundamentally estranged from the actual people living in the place they hoped to serve. They were cut off from meaningful relationship by a wall built out of their own self-referential visions and prevented from making meaningful contributions to the ultimate freedom of all the people by the limited scope of their own class-bound relationships.

The boldest and most influential nineteenth-century reformers were often similarly disconnected from the social context of their times. They too engaged in projects of reform while using their privilege to maintain a degree of paternalistic remove from the people and events they sought to change. Like Robert Owen, their loyalties often hewed to their own broad and abstract notions of progress rather than the actual needs of actual people in an unjust world.

At Brook Farm, the famed agrarian phalanx outside of Boston where Nathaniel Hawthorne famously raised a pitchfork back in

1841, the constitution of communal living enshrined their faithfulness to grand abstractions. It said, "We propose a radical and universal reform rather than to redress any particular wrong, or to remove the sufferings of any single class of human being."[67]

And so, the liberal church in the nineteenth century gave its heart to an abstraction.

In the twentieth century, fueled by an overwhelming force of American exceptionalism and the rising power of modernist thought, that faithfulness to grand abstractions was layered underneath a declarative triumphalism that made the liberal church believe all things were possible through our own moral advancement, even while failing to acknowledge that such advancement was continually centered around the experiences and ideals of privileged white people.

In the twenty-first century, accustomed to the preaching of this progressive good news and grounded in this historic faithfulness to grand abstractions, the liberal churches continue to expect liturgical triumphalism and social-action programming that delivers paternalistic aid for the people at the margins, even as the world cries out for something more.

The problem is not simply our optimism.

The problem is not even our hubris.

The problem is our continued estrangement. And the answer for this estrangement, while incomplete and messy and complicated in the extreme, has been there waiting for us all along.

It is, and has always been, relationship.

Relationality at Work

"What really makes you mad?" the community organizer asked me in my modestly decorated and neatly dusted church office. "I mean really, why exactly do you care?"

He was there, in the fall of 2006, to do a relational meeting because he wanted to know if I had leadership potential. To find that out, he needed to figure out who I was, what story I had to tell, and if I was capable of relating to people outside of my own limited scope of experience.

I told him I was angry that ministers in town got together once a month to plan the annual Thanksgiving interfaith service and pray rather blandly for the well-being of our congregants, all while immigrant children were being menaced at the school bus stops for the mere existence of their non-white faces.

I told him that if I had to sign another strongly worded letter to local legislators decrying the blatant racism of our civic discourse and policing practices, I was going to puke. I told him nobody cared about our strongly worded letters and I didn't care about our strongly worded letters and nothing the churches were doing was making a dent in the soul-crushing behemoth of xenophobia and white supremacy that was running rampant in our streets.

I told him I was angry that the religious community in our local jurisdiction was not capable of joining together to bring about authentic social change and, furthermore, did not seem to care that it was not capable of such mobilization. I told him I was angry at myself for participating in these pointless performances of collective compassion while not having the power to make a damn bit of difference.

So I guess I was mad about something.

And that was how I got into community organizing.

The key difference, I soon learned, between broad-based organizing and programs of benevolent service was the origin point of the work itself. In a broad-based community organization, the whole thing starts out in relationship and is fueled by a continual commitment to listening to each other's stories. Leadership then emerges not from the top of a hierarchical structure, but from the people most affected by the injustice we chose to face down together.

Instead of a bunch of pastors dropping into communities with programs of benevolent intent already worked out in our own heads, we learned how to show up at community centers, food pantries, bus stops, and service garages, armed with the singular intent of listening.

Through that listening, we built relationships of trust and accountability that put the people's stories at the center instead of gathering around the strategies laid out by all of us whom a patriarchal, supremacist society lifts up as leaders.

Community organizing can be hard and heartbreaking work. The false starts are innumerable. Sometimes (okay, more than sometimes) the white people still try to take over every room they enter. Often the men still talk over the women. Every day, somebody has to call somebody else out on their nonsense. And every day, in movements built around relationships of accountability, honest work is possible amid the dead utopias and broken dreams. Sometimes glory and grace present themselves in ways that even a full-time realist and part-time cynic such as me cannot ignore. Sometimes it is so beautiful that it brings me to my knees.

I am a clergy leader in the Industrial Areas Foundation, one of the largest broad-based organizing networks in the country. Since I live in the National Capital region, much of my work is connected to other lay and clergy leaders in and around Washington DC and Baltimore.

Often, I am brought by these leaders into the beauty and struggle of meaningful relationship even when I'm not ready for it. Often, these relationships mean that I am invited into some truly beautiful things even when I don't deserve it.

One of those gloriously meaningful and inherently relational things I have recently seen is a movement in Baltimore called Turnaround Tuesday. This program helps prepare previously incarcerated and unemployed citizens to reenter the workforce and step into transformational leadership in their communities.

That mission sounds safe enough. It's the kind of thing that many liberal leaders in many supposedly benevolent church or government programs could get behind. But the leaders at Turnaround Tuesday are adamant that they are not creating a program together.

It's not delivered from someone to someone else. It's not a grand abstract idea that just happens to affect the lives of real people. It's a movement, and the people who make up the movement are the people most deeply affected by its mission.

I recently visited Turnaround Tuesday on one of the hundreds of afternoons in which the leaders and emerging leaders have gathered in a church basement in Baltimore. There were over a hundred formerly incarcerated returning citizens and job searchers gathered together for the 9:00 A.M. start time.

A smattering of organizers, pastors, parole officers, and community leaders were hanging around. An actual billionaire was present, invited just like the rest of us to participate in the day's activities but not to direct them. And there was me, present in part to help handle the billionaire, but also there to be reminded of just what it feels like to momentarily escape the persistent estrangement from which we all suffer.

The meeting started right on time. We didn't mess around for long before getting to the meat and potatoes of the issue. A woman sitting near the front, whom we'll call Penny, volunteered to get the whole thing started. When she rose to read the statement of higher purpose the participants had agreed upon, she did it forcefully, without hesitation or a single break in her voice.

"Your misery is your ministry," Penny said. "Your pain is your purpose. Your suffering is your service. Your mess becomes your Message. Your test becomes your testimony. God allows us to hurt to heal others, because you cannot heal what you cannot feel. So, don't let the pain of your past punish your present and paralyze your progress and purpose."

Amen, I thought.

And then we were instructed to turn to face the person next to us and tell something essential about our own story. "Don't be afraid of your own story," the facilitators reminded us. "Your story is where your power is at."

At Turnaround Tuesday, the stories, experiences, suffering, and exaltation of the people are the very substance of the movement itself.

Turnaround Tuesday has done what no safely distant institution of benign reform could ever do. It's changed people's lives not in concept, but in form. In three years, the movement has connected more than 366 people to living-wage jobs, and, over the course of those three years, the participants in the process have repeatedly become its leaders.

That morning, I was reminded that it is not the liberal church that is the object of my highest commitment, but relationship itself, facilitated and amplified by the progressive congregation I serve. Relationship is my religion, through and through, and when a commitment to authentic relational engagement is present in liberal religion, then I am exactly where I belong.

I was right where I belonged at Turnaround Tuesday, especially after we told our stories and worked through some basic job readiness skills, all one hundred of us pushing aside the chairs, kicking off our shoes, and rather oddly but beautifully gathering together to do fifteen minutes of aerobic exercises.

You see, the participants and leaders had deemed that transformation wasn't wholly possible without engaging body, mind, and spirit. So the founding pastor of the movement, one of the most powerful men in the city of Baltimore, put on some track pants and walked us through an exercise video, all while calling out the names of people in the room and laughing so hard I thought he might cry.

A man and woman in well-greased wheelchairs flanked the floor with rolling enthusiasm. Nobody really listened to the weirdly peppy music. The people who could twirl surely twirled. Penny, whose eldest child no longer spoke to her after the long stint she spent in prison, really did dance like nobody was watching.

I stepped into the fray with the billionaire on my right-hand side and a recent parolee who served sixteen years for second-degree manslaughter on my left. We moved, kicked, laughed, and tripped together—and in that moment, nobody in that room was trying to be anybody else's savior. And nobody was asking to be saved by anybody else's grand ideals.

Truly beautiful things are possible when we relate as equals. Grace moves when we stop being distantly paternalistic and start being human.

As we tripped over each other at Turnaround Tuesday, the fundamental estrangement we have known—that which separates us from ourselves, from the holy, and from each other—slipped away. For a moment, we were whole.

Which is not to say that we were not broken, or that we were all going to make it out alive. Which is not to say that we wouldn't fail one another, or that we had forgotten what hurt us. Which is not to say that all our plans would come to fruition, or that the arc of the universe would just keep bending eternally toward justice, starting right there in that Baltimore church basement.

It is only to say that we were not fooling ourselves. And we were not hiding from change. And we were choosing to love actual persons instead of abstract ideals.

The Opposite of Certainty

Some measure of estrangement may be part of the human experience. We may not be able to banish it altogether any more than we could cultivate carefully studied moral perfection. Tillich thought that we are always pulled between our dependence on others and the astonishing hubris that compels us to place our own selves at the center of the universe. In this tug of war between estrangement and mutuality, the race may never be fully run.

Still, this does not mean that we should simply stop moving. Just because we are honest does not mean we cannot be hopeful. As Václav Havel famously articulated, hope is not just another version of optimism. Optimism tells a preordained narrative. It is an assertion that the scales have already been tipped toward triumph. Optimism is always busy absolving somebody.

Hope is different. Like faith, hope is the exact opposite of certainty. It does not presume an outcome for good or for ill. It lies in the waiting moment when the tug from both directions is not yet fully resolved and when a great many things are still possible. It moves in the humble spaces that open when we allow ourselves to be uncertain and thus not fully self-contained. It is the possibility, though not the inevitability, of a better way.

Philosopher Hannah Arendt declares, "Even in the darkest of times we have the right to expect some illumination . . . [a light that] some men and women, in their lives and works, will kindle under almost all circumstances and shed over the time span that was given them on earth."[68]

We have the right to expect some illumination, even in the shadow of the dead utopias. Even if we cannot expect to stand in the sunshine of pure promise, we can expect that both hope and meaning are evident in our interconnected lives. We are bound always to the ground of our being, the truth of our deepest selves, and the network of accountability we form with one another.

My grandma, who lived her life in a state of estrangement from the good and respectable people of the church, expected and received illumination from the people who chose to relate meaningfully to her throughout her life.

Leaders of color within and outside of liberal religion, facing the estrangement caused by the centering of whiteness, find illumination when connected to one another and to all those who are committed enough to acknowledge the fullness of their stories.

Generation X ministers struggling to define our own way forward in a postmodern age still seek and find relational connection within the life of our congregations. We find illumination when we join the ones we serve in asking age-old questions in whole new ways.

Hope does not require ease. It does not require naiveté. It is real, tangible, and enduring—even after the good news has all been declared—even when the authentic stories of our lives do not have fairy-tale happy beginnings, middles, or ends.

Appendix A

On Prayers of Confession or Atonement

Atonement can be a painful and complicated concept for liberal worshippers. Sometimes the way we feel about it is deeply affected by our previous religious experiences of guilt and shame. Sometimes the whole thing just seems unpleasant.

More than anything, atonement makes us feel vulnerable. It asks us to go to places we might rather avoid. It is not for the faint of heart or for fragile relationships. The work—whatever it may be—proceeds at the pace of trust. It does not and cannot proceed faster.

And so, any engagement with atonement theology has to begin within circles of trust. Small group ministries and dedicated spiritual circles are good places to begin. Start small. Build safety. Make respectful room for vulnerability. Then see where the practice of shared atonement in your community takes you.

For most congregations in my Unitarian Universalist tradition, a regular practice of shared atonement in the main worship service currently would not be viable. The trust and vulnerability in the Sunday service often simply can't be achieved in a group of several hundred people. But imagine if at least a hundred of those people had previously gone deep in these discussions in their own small groups. Imagine if the liturgy wasn't led or lorded over by clergy alone, but shared in fellowship with lay leaders. Imagine what it would take to pray words of honest atonement with one another. Could your minister read a prayer like the one that follows on a Sunday morning? Could you? Could I? How could we build the trust to make such an honest prayer possible among us?

Sample Prayer

God of all—that which is within us, among us, and beyond us—

In the busy rush between one day and the next,
we confess to the casual indifference of each street corner passing;
the self-protective stance of each missed opportunity for compassion.

In worship, we prepare our hearts to reach again for that shining
    moment—
When, for once, we raise our eyes
from the scuffs on our shoes,
the gum on the sidewalk,
the companionship of expectantly hovering obligations
and see there, looking back, the eyes of a stranger who sees a stranger,
transformed from an obstacle
into a human being
through the pervasive magic of an encounter.

God of all, spirit of hope—
Help us to remember that,
though we have fallen short,
though we have broken our vows,
though we have sinned in what we have done
and in what we have failed to do,
we are connected to you, and to one another,
by a redeeming mutuality that both heals and demands,
that gives comfort amid the holy agitation of our days.

Help us to see one another,
really see one another's pressing hurt and uplifting joy
and to answer those joys and those sorrows
with every tool of transformation.

Together, may we be both knowing and known,
seen and believed,
companions on the journey—
created, imperfect, and committed.

May it be so.
Amen.

Appendix B

On Liturgies of Lament

Over beers at a bar, I once looked at my progressive Episcopalian friend with liturgical envy in my eyes. "You've got it all," I said. "It's all right there—in Holy Week—if you pay attention."

The whole arc of suffering, relationship, forgiveness, and hope is written across the span of one single week of the Christian calendar. From Palm Sunday, when all things are possible, to Good Friday, when the altar is draped in darkness, to the glory of Easter morning.

Right in the middle of it is a service I have only once experienced in a Unitarian Universalist context—the Tenebrae, the purest liturgy of lament I have ever known. The liturgy of the Tenebrae (Latin for "darkness" or "shadow") is often observed on Thursday or Friday of Holy Week and dates back more than a thousand years. In it, gospel readings detailing the last hours of Jesus' life are shared one at a time while candles are successively extinguished. The service ends in darkness.

The light does not return until the worshippers do, when the dawn breaks at Easter. For this one service both the silence and the darkness are sustained, just as the loss and the suffering of the story are sustained. Nothing is glossed over or hurried through.

Adaptations of the traditional Tenebrae service have often included readings and reflections on the sufferings of contemporary society. Such services can be difficult, beautiful, and searing. There are plenty of examples. Just tap it in your search engine. It's all right there, in Holy Week—the whole sweep of human emotion.

I've never had to go searching for liturgies of lament, though. Just as it's all right there in the span of Holy Week, it's all right there in the life of the congregations I have served as well.

We don't have to go looking for tragedy. We don't have to mourn in abstraction. Grief finds us. And whether we are ready or not, observances of that grief demand our care and attention.

Virginia Tech. Sandy Hook. Pulse Nightclub in Orlando. The murder of Michael Brown. The death-dealing violence of white nationalists in Charlottesville. Teenagers gone too soon. Gun violence in our own families.

We don't have to go looking. We just have to show up, because ignoring it would be faithless.

I've shown up and built observances for far too many such moments in our collective lives as congregations and as a nation. I will be asked to do it again. I really don't have answers, but I do have a few lessons learned and one small example.

When crafting liturgies of lament, here are some things to consider:

- **Be ready.** The turn-around time from searing loss to liturgical marking of that loss is usually very fast. Prepare your heart. Do not be surprised.
- **Start with the music.** Music is the quickest way to the heart, and live music is the most important element of an authentic liturgy of lament. Sometimes it is the only element you really need. Sometimes it is only a single drum. Powerful music doesn't have to be complicated music.
- **Do not ascribe meaning to everything.** Not yet. Just as the Tenebrae service ends in darkness, sometimes we need to acknowledge the pain before we ascribe an orderly meaning to it. Leave in the darkness. Come back to the light.
- **Consider caucusing.** Usually there are some among us who are more vulnerable and vastly more affected than others. When LGBTQIA people are targeted or harmed, LGBTQIA people need to be together in that grief. When a teenager dies, the youth

group needs their space to mourn. Different identity groups may in fact need wholly different rituals. Be prepared to listen to and make space for those differences.

- **Pivot to commitment instead of hope.** Hope will come. It will. But in the immediate context of loss and lament, people yearn to feel less powerless. Liturgy can invite commitment as a way of claiming power. In a liturgy mourning the loss of life in an epidemic of gun violence, worshippers can be invited to one small act of advocacy for common sense gun laws. When LGBTQIA siblings are wounded and oppressed, funding and volunteerism can be gathered for local service organizations that foster equal rights and protections. Don't feel like you have to prescribe that commitment for people, just open a space for it where you can.

- **Get creative if you can do it authentically.** But not if you feel like you have to. I've gathered grieving people around bowls of dry leaves, life crumbling to bits in their fingers. I've sat on the floor of our sanctuary with my head in my hands while thirty yards of red fabric waved anxiously behind me. I've beckoned people to sprinkle salt into clear water, a symbol of our tears. And sometimes I've just shown up, stood around the piano, and listened. Do what feels authentic, nothing more, and certainly nothing less.

- **Cry later.** Really. When everyone has gone home, when the candles are all extinguished, cry then. And know what an honor it is to build a liturgy that touches your own soul too.

Sample Liturgy

In one of the deadliest mass shootings in U.S. history, 32 people died after being gunned down on the campus of Virginia Tech by Seung Hui Cho, a student at the college who later committed suicide. At the time, I served a congregation in Northern Virginia, and a number of young adults within our community witnessed the events. When we prepared this vigil, we had just received confirmation that the Virginia Tech students connected to our congregation had survived. Only hours before, we were not certain.

Vigil of Lament: Virginia Tech Shootings, April 2007

Music for Gathering—live piano music, able to stretch based on changing attendance. Also played quietly under Opening Words.

Opening Words

We, whose journeys are always beginning
we, whose mission always awaits us
we, whose visions are bent on loving,
we gather together here.
We gather as a community drawn together out of common need.
We gather together with questions—the kinds of questions that have
no easy answers.
We gather with hope that pulses on through untold suffering.
We gather with tenderness for one another that can only be known
from knowing human blessings and human failures.

Our grief is holy ground,
And so we gather on this holy ground, thirsting and hungry for
meaning,
drawn to the source of all weeping, all devotion, and all grace.
In this quiet time, may we who are hungry and sorrowful find nour-
ishment and rest.

Silence Until Music Ends

Thirty-three people, with loves and losses and hopes and dreams, 33
people whose lives moved in the tide of the universe until ripples of
their presence were felt by everyone, everywhere, for each life touches
every other, and we are never alone. We are never isolated. We are
one family, and this evening we mourn the loss of 33 members of
our beloved human family, 33 living treasures now gone on to the
mystery.

We gather to remember them, to mourn them, to mourn the
tragic desperation that led to their deaths. We gather to remind ourselves that such desperation, such isolation, such sorrow as this, is
not an inevitability in this world, but a persistent reality, held with-

in a larger truth—that we are but one human family, connected in mystery and wonder, in joy and in sorrow, to one another and to the source from which we come and to which, in mystery, we all return. We are connected to them—to the ones we have lost, and to one another, here in the midst of our lamentation.

Candles of Remembrance—lit one by one, as the name of each victim is read aloud, with silence in between

Prayer
Spirit of life and love, you who move within us, among us and beyond us,
We offer up the flickering lights of these small candles, remembrances of those whose loss weighs so heavily on our hearts.
We hear their names and we see the images of sorrow and hurt around the world, and we reach out for the hope that lies beneath what our eyes can see and our ears can hear.
Help us to respond to our outrage with commitment instead of fear.
Help us to come up out of our sorrow with renewed strength.
Help us to move through our confusion with the conviction that we can make of this broken world a place of purpose, of faithfulness, of dedication for each and every heart that still beats, starting with our own.
Spirit of love, meet us once again in our brokenness and guide us toward the path of peace.
May it be so, and Amen.

Music for Reflection and Silent Candle Lighting—vocal performance of the traditional African-American spiritual "Wade in the Water"

Benediction
And now, though sorrow and pain abide,
let us gather what strength we have,
what confidence and valor and faith—

for we live to tell the story of our days—
and in this telling,
as in this weeping,
we are not alone,
but connected in mystery and wonder,
through the veil of our own pain—
to ourselves, to each other, and to all that remains holy,
even in times such as these.
May it be so, and Amen.

Notes

1. Daniel Berrigan, *The Dark Night of Resistance* (Eugene, OR: Wipf and Stock, 2007), p. 4.

2. A reference to the popular hymn "We'll Build a Land," by Barbara Zanotte (words) and Carolyn McDade (music).

3. This oft-cited quote from Martin Luther King is derived from a sermon given by Unitarian and abolitionist Theodore Parker in 1853. In that sermon, Parker said, "I do not pretend to understand the moral universe. The arc is a long one. My eye reaches but little ways. I cannot calculate the curve and complete the figure by experience of sight. I can divine it by conscience. And from what I see I am sure it bends toward justice."

4. Berrigan, *The Dark Night of Resistance*, p. 17.

5. Chris Jennings, *Paradise Now: The Story of American Utopianism* (New York: Random House, 2016), p. 106.

6. Thomas Carlyle, *The Correspondence of Thomas Carlyle and Ralph Waldo Emerson, 1834–1872*, Vol. 1 (Scotts Valley, CA: Create Space, 2018), p. 54.

7. A.L. Morton, *The Life and Ideas of Robert Owen* (New York: International Publishers, 1962), p. 73.

8. Ibid., p. 75.

9. Ralph Waldo Emerson, *The Collected Works of Ralph Waldo Emerson, Volume V: English Traits.* Phillip Nicoloff, Robert Burkholder, Emory Douglas Wilson (eds.) (Boston: Harvard University Press, 1994), p. 330.

10. Charles Sotheran, *Horace Greeley, and Other Pioneers of American Socialism* (New York: The Humboldt Publishing Company, 1892), p. 73.

11. From display at the Atheneum/Visitors Center, New Harmony, Indiana.

12 Joseph Clayton, *Robert Owen: Pioneer of Social Reforms* (London: A.C. Fitfield, 1908), p. 43.

13 A. Powell Davies, "America's Real Religion" in Dan McKanan (ed.), *A Documentary History of Unitarian Universalism, Volume Two: From 1900 to the Present* (Boston: Skinner House Books, 2017), p. 156.

14 Tom Schade, "There Is No Going Back," *UU World*, Fall 2016.

15 A. Powell Davies, in *A Documentary History*, p. 156.

16 Pankaj Mishra, *Age of Anger: A History of the Present* (New York: Farrar, Strauss and Giroux, 2017), pp. 82–114.

17 Rebecca Parker and Rita Nakashima Brock, *Saving Paradise: How Christianity Traded Love of This World for Crucifixion and Empire* (Boston: Beacon Press, 2008) pp. 394–395.

18 James Luther Adams, *On Being Human Religiously: Selected Essays in Religion and Society,* 2nd Edition, Max Stackhouse (ed.) (Boston: Beacon Press, 1976), p. 8.

19 Steven Pinker, "Science Is Not Your Enemy," *The New Republic*, August 6, 2013.

20 This insight gleaned from a longer, more thoughtful exposition of the point in Paul Rasor, *Faith Without Certainty: Liberal Theology in the Twentieth Century* (Boston: Skinner House Books, 2005), p. 40.

21 Zadie Smith, "On Optimism and Despair," *The New York Review of Books*, December 22, 2016.

22 David Remnick, "Obama Reckons with a Trump Presidency," *The New Yorker*, November 28, 2016.

23 Zadie Smith, "On Optimism and Despair."

24 Paul Kingsnorth, "2016: Year of the Serpent," dark-mountain.net, December, 2016.

25 Paul Kingsnorth and Hine Dougald, *Dark Mountain Manifesto* dark-mountain.net/about/manifesto.

26 Ta-Nehisi Coates, "The First White President," *The Atlantic*, October 2017.

27 Touré, "White People Explain Why They Feel Oppressed," *Vice*, September 17, 2015. Lecture.

28 W.E.B. DuBois, *Darkwater: Voices from Within the Veil*. E-book #15210 (Project Gutenberg, February 28, 2005).

29 Miguel De La Torre, "Toward a Theology of Hopelessness." Blog post, drmigueldelatorre.com/2015/toward-a-theology-of-hopelessness, March 14, 2015.

30 Ibid.

31 Ibid.

32 From personal conversation.

33 T.S. Eliot, *The Rock: A Pageant Play* (New York: Harcourt, Brace, Jovanovich, 1934), p. 42.

34 Douglas E. Oakman, *Jesus and the Peasants* (Eugene, Oregon: Cascade Books, 2008), p. 114.

35 Rebecca Ann Parker, *Blessing the World: What Will Save Us Now*, Robert Hardies (ed.) (Boston: Skinner House Books, 2016), pp. 25–26.

36 Ibid., p. 26.

37 Barbara Brown Taylor, *An Altar in the World: Finding the Sacred Beneath Our Feet* (London: Canterbury Press, 2009), p. 93.

38 James Luther Adams, *On Being Human Religiously*, p. 37.

39 James Luther Adams, "The Changing Reputation of Human Nature," in *The Essential James Luther Adams: Selected Essays and Addresses*, George Kimmich Beach (ed.) (Boston: Skinner House Books, 1998), p. 61.

40 Ibid., p. 66.

41 James Luther Adams, "A Little Lower Than the Angels," in *The Prophethood of All Believers*, George Kimmich Beach (ed.) (Boston: Beacon Press, 1986), p. 180.

42 Bryan Sevenson, Ware Lecture. Unitarian Universalist Association General Assembly, June 24, 2017.

43 From personal conversation.

44 Chimamanda Ngozi Adichie, "Now Is the Time to Talk About What We Are Actually Talking About," *The New Yorker*, December 2, 2016.

45 Marjorie Hewitt Suchocki, *The Fall to Violence, Original Sin in Relational Theology* (New York: Continuum, 1995), pp. 82–100.

46 Ibid.

47 Molly Housh Gordon, "From Tethers of Captivity to Roots of Flourishing: Collective Sin and Mutual Struggle in the Web that Connects Us." Unpublished paper, Prairie Group, November 2015.

48 Anthony B. Pinn, *The End of God Talk: An African American Humanist Theology* (Oxford: Oxford University Press, 2012), pp. 44–45.

49 Bryan Stevenson, Lecture. Gadsden State Community College, September 2, 2016.

50 Kilian McDonnell, *Swift, Lord, You Are Not* (Collegeville, MN: St. John's University Press, 2003).

51 Sean Parker Dennison, "Mission Impossible: Why Failure Is Not an Option," Lecture, The 195th Ministerial Conference at Berry Street, June 2015.

52 David Lambert, "Repent, Trump!: The Problem with Apology," religiondispatches.org, October 20, 2016.

53 Ashley Horan, "Ten Commandments for Relevant, Reparative Ministry: A Reinterpretation of the Hebrew Scriptures for Those of Us Who Are White," Lecture, 197th Ministerial Conference at Berry Street, June 2017.

54 Jason Shelton, "The Lost Art of Confession," Sermon, First Unitarian Universalist Church of Nashville, March 26, 2017.

55 Dov Peretz Elkins (ed.), *Yom Kippur Readings: Inspiration, Information and Contemplation* (Woodstock, VT: Jewish Lights Publishing, 2010), p. 43.

56 Rob Eller-Isaacs, "Unforgiven," Unpublished Paper, Prairie Group, March 5, 2017, p. 9.

57 James Baldwin, *Notes of a Native Son* (Boston: Beacon Press, 1955), p. 101.

58 Vogt, V.O., *Modern Worship* (New Haven, CT: Yale University Press, 1927), p. 2. The quotation appears to be a paraphrase of Guy Allan Tawney, "Religion and Experimentation," *International Journal of Ethics*, Vol. 36, No. 4 (July, 1926), pp. 337–356.

59 William Wallace Fenn, "Modern Liberalism," *American Journal of Theology* 17 (October 1913), p. 516.

60 James Weldon Johnson, *Saint Peter Relates an Incident: Selected Poems* (New York: Viking Press, 1935).

61 Joseph R. Winters, *Hope Draped in Black: Race, Melancholy and the Agony of Progress* (Durham, NC: Duke University Press, 2016), p. 16.

62 Shane Paul Neil, "The Offensiveness of My Pain," Unitarian Universalist Association WorshipWeb, uua.org/worship/words/reflection/offensiveness-my-pain. Used with permission.

63 Mitra Rahnema (ed.), *Centering: Navigating Race, Authenticity, and Power in Ministry* (Boston: Skinner House Books, 2017), p. 178.

64 Thomas G. Long and Cornelius Plantinga, Jr. (eds.), *A Chorus of Witnesses: Model Sermons for Today's Preacher* (Grand Rapids, MI: Eerdmans, 1994), p. 98.

65 Paul Tillich, "Estranged and Reunited: The New Being," Sermon, delivered at the dedication of the Roofless Church, New Harmony, Indiana, June 2, 1963.

66 Eric Reece, *Utopia Drive: A Road Trip Through America's Most Radical Idea* (New York: Farrar, Straus and Giroux, 2016), p. 111.

67 Joel Myerson (ed.), *Transcendentalism: A Reader* (Oxford: Oxford University Press, 2000), p. 465.

68 Hannah Arendt, *Men in Dark Times* (New York: Harcourt, Brace and Company, 1968), p. ix.